MARIA EDGEWORTH

MARIA EDGEWORTH

by

P. H. NEWBY

ENGLISH NOVELISTS SERIES

ARTHUR BARKER LTD.

30 MUSEUM STREET, LONDON, W.C.1

FOR D. W. J.

First published 1950

PRINTED IN GREAT BRITAIN BY
MORRISON AND GIBB LTD., LONDON AND EDINBURGH

MARIA EDGEWORTH

THE death of the novel has been announced on several occasions during the past two hundred years. The first was probably round about the year 1770. Fielding and Richardson appeared to have achieved everything of which the novel was capable, Smollett and Sterne were regarded as marking the beginning of a period of decadence and, when they were gone, it was hard to see just where and how any fresh development was possible. The novel was in the hands of the Grub Street hacks and the fair authoresses. As late as 1790 the *Monthly Review* pronounced that the manufacture of novels had been so long established that they had arrived at mediocrity.

Fair authoresses were regarded as a race apart. When their work came into the hands of the gentlemanly reviewer he examined it chiefly for spelling mistakes and errors of grammatical construction. There are a number of kind things that one would like to say about these ladies, but unfortunately most of them would be untrue : it is not true, for example, that even in Fanny Burney do we find any deeper under-standing of feminine nature than was shown by Richardson. Feeling that they were in print only on sufferance, under the protection of anonymity or a husband's foreword, they set about portraying women as it was thought proper for men to know them. It could hardly be expected of young ladies who had taken to the writing of novels because, in comparison with other forms of literature, it seemed so easy that they should be capable of the gusto for realism

5

which would have been necessary to portray women as they really are. And the rest was satire and morality.

How heavily moral they were can be illustrated by a characteristic remark of one of them, Clara Reeve : " The great and important duty of a writer is to point out the difference between virtue and vice, to show one as rewarded and the other as punished."

The tone of all eighteenth-century literature is moralistic but never so nakedly moralistic as in the hands of the earnest blue-stockings in the closing decades of the century. They were usually educationists, charged with the bringing up of younger brothers and sisters, great readers of Locke, Rousseau and the more informative memoirs and travel books. And if their books were starched with moral instruction they had the compensation of living what appear, at this distance, to be singularly happy lives. Their sprightliness and good humour went not so much into their books as into the art of living. Who, for example, would have suspected that Mrs. Barbauld once climbed an apple-tree and swung over the garden wall in order to escape from a too-ardent suitor ? And if their heroines were passive creatures living under the rule of Prudence it was a word that had a different ring to the eighteenth-century ear. Even the great Fielding con- sidered it the quality without which " if a man does not become a felon to the world, he is at least *felo de se*." The new heroine was constantly on her guard against the delusions of romance and the treachery of her own warm heart. As a character in Mrs. James Keir's *History of Miss Greville* put it, he would wish his wife to feel passion but not to express it, since the turbulence of passion is incompatible with " that inner delicacy . . . which is inseparable from a truly virtuous female mind." The once loving husband can run away with the foreign countess if he likes, but it is the woman's part to suffer in silence uncomplainingly until the nobility of her character is so manifest that he returns and throws himself at her feet. The new heroine was prudent to the point of coldness, something of a blue-stocking and frequently gifted with a morbid longing to sacrifice her own welfare for what she fallaciously imagined to be the good of others. Fielding's young woman had developed into Charlotte Smith's young lady.

If this were all what dull books they would have been. The truth is, of course, that the novels were lively even under the deadweight of a prudent and passive miss. The fair authoresses passed easily from moral reflection to an uninhibited enjoyment of the lighter side of life, a transition that (as compared with the Victorians) was all the easier for them because they were not obsessed by the guilt-consciousness that makes morality so tedious. Their most deadly weapon was their sense of the ridiculous and their surest target those masculine qualities which arose as the result of man's assumption of the subjection of women : the boorishness of the country squire who brought his hounds into the drawing-room, the ignorance of the packs of men who warmed their seats at the drawing-room fire with their coat tails turned up, the self-satisfaction of the obviously undesirable suitor making a proposal of marriage to a young lady he expects to swoon with gratitude. (Jane Austen's Mr. Collins comes of a long lineage.)

The literary expression of so much refinement undoubtedly corresponded to a real change that was coming over society towards the end of the century. Squire Western has given up his hounds, his drink and his cursing, he had brought Sophia up to town where she is put in the care of an elderly aunt who is one of the leading show-women in the great marriage circus. This is where the fair authoresses came into their own. If convention prevented the heroine from being anything but demure there was scope for the presentation of a dragoness in her aunt and plenty of space could be devoted to the semi-military tactics of match-making. It was an opportunity that they just failed to take. Fanny Burney became Madame D'Arblay and, although she was anticipated, no Madame de Lafayette arose. There were chill winds of theory in the elegant corridors and the brilliant candelabras flickered. The fair authoresses sat patiently embroidering texts supplied by Rousseau or, more frequently, the endemic Puritanism, and the silliest of them dwelt upon the pleasures and pains of excessive sensibility.

They were anything but realists. Too many of the fair authoresses saw in the novel a means of indulging themselves in flights of ideal pleasure as a compensation for their own unexciting lives, or of ideal revenge in the form of satire on those features of society which had caused them humiliation. But they were clever enough not to stray outside their own field. Action went on in the boudoir and the ballroom, in country houses and fashionable watering-places. We see the menfolk coming in from their hunting or dressed for dinner, we see them at the door on the way to the club or the counting-house, or carried in dying but vociferous from the duelling ground. The great wide world was appraised by its reflection in a cup of tea. Heroes and heroines blushed alike and there was fainting at the click of a patch-box. And, with such rare exceptions as the novels of Charlotte Smith, even the tradespeople and servants were never anything but lay figures.

This was the novel of manners as Maria Edgeworth and

Jane Austen found it. Jane Austen did little to extend its field—her chosen limitations enabled her to perfect an art—and we do not follow the menfolk to their affairs in the City nor listen to the tittle-tattle of servants. Unlike her predecessors, however, she was not interested in idealised characters who blushed or fainted their way into what were, basically, false predicaments, and a great deal of her creative drive came from fun at the expense of the popular fiction of the circulating libraries. But she was something more than a satirist : she was, and it was for this quality that her contemporaries found her so refreshing, a realist.

There were those, it is true, who could accept realism only if it was accompanied by moral uplift and the lack of it in Jane Austen caused her works to be thought a little insipid. " What do you think of *Mansfield Park* ? " we find Lady Anne Romilly writing to Maria Edgeworth in 1814. " It has been pretty generally admired here and I think all novels must be that are true to life which this is, with a good story vein of principle running thro' the whole. It has not, however, that elevation of virtue, something beyond nature, that gives the greatest charm to a novel, but it is a natural everyday life and will amuse an idle hour in spite of its faults."

Having regard to the kind of novel that *Mansfield Park* is, Lady Romilly's remarks are a curiosity of criticism. They were made, of course, with the Maria Edgeworth kind of novel in mind, they were intended as a little oblique flattery. For although Maria Edgeworth was a realist of the order of Jane Austen, the impulse lying behind a great deal of what she wrote was too frequently " that elevation of virtue, something beyond nature " which transformed the artist's vision of life into the moralist's warning. Yet she was a

genuinely creative writer. She took over the novel of
manners as one of the perquisites of her sex, reinvigorated it
with the breath of life (her *Belinda*, 1801, precedes the
publication of Jane Austen's novels by several years and
gave clear evidence of a fresh, realistic response to what
might have been stale material) and, if we admit her moral
purpose, she nevertheless extended the range of fiction as it
had up to that time been written by women. She took her
readers not only to the country house but also into the
doctor's consulting room, to the officers' mess, to the young
lawyer's rooms in one of the Inns of Court and, most important of all, she took them into the cabin of the Irish
peasant, found material that she made peculiarly her own
and, in so doing, gave dignity to the regional subject and
made the regional novel possible.

But there is only one way of approaching Maria Edgeworth. Because of the extraordinary influence he wielded
over his daughter's mind we have, first of all, to make the
acquaintance of her father. Richard Lovell Edgeworth was
a clarety-complexioned, opinionated, never silent Irish
country gentleman with a passion for mechanics, for
education and for matrimony. He married four times if
we except a curious mock-marriage that took place at a
party when he was fifteen and which his father (who appears
to have taken the matter much more seriously than it
warranted) had annulled by a suit of jactitation in the
ecclesiastical court. Edgeworth's first regular marriage was
with Anna Maria Elers, a union that took place while he
was still an undergraduate at Oxford. Even before the
marriage he had, it appears, very little affection for the
unfortunate lady and only made her his wife because, having
" engaged her affections " he could see no other course open

to him that was consistent with his strong sense of honour ; and during her lifetime he showed such admiration for more alluring female company that, on one occasion, the wife of Dr. Erasmus Darwin had to pull him up at the dinner table by proposing the health of the absent Mrs. Edgeworth.

It was this first wife who became, in 1767, the mother of Maria. Within a few months of her death in 1773 he married the beautiful and celebrated Honora Sneyd, for whatever criticisms there might be of Edgeworth it could never be said that he lacked success with the ladies. Was he not the best dancer in England ? Like nearly everything he did this second marriage proved a great success, and before she died in 1780 Honora had gained such an understanding of his nature that she strongly recommended him to marry her sister Elizabeth. Edgeworth was impressed by this shrewdness and eight months later proceeded to the marriage that Honora had proposed. Although considered highly scandalous this marriage also turned out most happily and when, in 1797, Elizabeth died in her turn Edgeworth found himself on such good terms with himself that he thought it fitting to marry Frances Beaufort, the daughter of a local clergyman, a woman who was two years younger than Maria, his own daughter. By his four wives he had no less than twenty-two children, only four of whom died in infancy, and it was not the least of Edgeworth's achievements that they, together with the two spinster sisters of Honora and Elizabeth, contrived to live together in complete accord in the rambling country mansion house of Edgeworthstown—a house that is situated in flat, rather uninteresting country some sixty miles north-west of Dublin.

To Richard Lovell Edgeworth life presented a number of problems but few mysteries. Although officially a

Protestant (an important circumstance in Ireland) he cannot be called a religious man. Lacking spiritual depth his mind turned to other problems than those of faith. One, for example, was the construction of a carriage on a new principle : " that, in turning round, it continued to stand on four points, nearly at equal distances from one another ; whereas in carriages with a crane neck, when the four wheels are *locked* under the perch, the fore-carriage is very unsteady, being supported on only three points." It was a problem that he solved to his complete satisfaction, and the resulting phaeton was approved by the Society for the Encouragement of the Arts. He made clocks, he invented a sailing-carriage, patented a signalling apparatus which he called a telegraph, tried to construct a wooden horse that would jump over stone walls (he almost invented the caterpillar track in doing so), built a new spire for the village church and had it hauled to the top of the tower by rope and pulley while one of his sons played on a bugle, is regarded by some people as the father of modern road-making, and filled his house at Edgeworthstown with gadgets and contrivances so that for decades after his death unwary guests were trapped in their rooms by complex locks that only members of the family knew how to deal with.

There were other, and perhaps more solid, achievements. He placed the administration of his Irish estates on such sound footing that, years after his death, they were weathering times of stress while neighbouring landowners were going into bankruptcy. Having such a large family he very sensibly set about considering the principles of education, and he has earned respectful mention in histories of pedagogy because he arrived at the enlightened conclusion that true education could only be based upon a deeper understanding of the needs and nature of the child mind, an understanding to be obtained by treating the subject as an experimental science in which the conversation and acts of children should be noted down. His belief in education was unbounded. He attempted to rear his first son as an English Emile and the boy was actually presented to Rousseau for examination. The experiment was, however, a failure and the boy proved so stubborn that nothing could be done with him except by his father. Edgeworth was considerably disillusioned. But the rather rigid contemporary and orthodox views on education were permanently enlivened for him by all that was most warming in the ideals of Rousseauism ; and, at Edgeworthstown, at least, the dreary deification of the Useful became an education that was based upon the natural curiosity of the child. " No tears ! " was his cry. " No tasks ! No masters ! Nothing upon compulsion ! "

Life, death, education, love and literature came up for his inspection and proved to be problems of no greater difficulty than had been the invention of a one-wheel coach. He solved them with a smile upon his face. And in these instances he had no need of the approbation of the Society for the Encouragement of the Arts : he received it wholeheartedly from his own family and especially from Maria. He had the frank and open disposition of a supremely confident man. Such difficulties as he had were made the common property of the family. Secrecy and reserve were unknown to him. Before his fourth marriage nothing could be more natural than the way he announced the news to Maria. " He threw open his whole mind to me—let me see all the changes and workings of his heart . . . the consequence was that no daughter ever felt more sympathy with a father than I felt for him." His sons wrote to him as from one friend to another and it was his proudest boast that not one tear per month was shed in his house nor the voice of reproof heard nor the hand of restraint felt.

Perhaps he owed as much to his family as his family owed to him. Family responsibility helps to keep a man from eccentricity, and although there have been many who have called him a crank we have only to compare him with his greatest friend, Mr. Thomas Day, to see what real eccentricity could achieve. Day was the author of the once-famous *Sandford and Merton* and had, with Edgeworth, been a member of the interesting scientific and literary coterie that had forgathered during the 'seventies at Lichfield under the leadership of Dr. Erasmus Darwin and Anne Seward. Day was wealthy, he was a bachelor and there was nothing to give check to the luxuriant growth of his fancy. While Edgeworth put Rousseau's ideas to practical test and found they did not work Day became the most advanced and certainly the silliest follower of Rousseau in England. Day thought long and hard about marriage, paid solemn attentions to Honora and Elizabeth Sneyd who were then living at Lichfield, but his suit did not prosper. Edgeworth, with his great practical bent, married them, both of them. And he was much too ardent a creature ever to have carried out Day's celebrated experiment in wife-rearing.

Day was so offended by the corruption of society that the only woman he could think of marrying was one reared and educated by himself. To this end two girls were selected. Some authorities say that the spare one was being reared for a friend, others that two were chosen as a guarantee of success. They were educated in " simplicity, perfect innocence and attachment to " Mr. Day. The first girl, however, proved invincibly stupid and was married off to a small shopkeeper. The second, although very pretty, showed a lamentable fondness for ribbons and other frivolities. What is more, she failed to come up to Mr. Day's rather high standards of fortitude ; when he dropped hot sealing wax upon her arm or fired pistols into her petticoats she would insist on screaming. So Day had to marry an heiress like any other mortal.

It was, of course, an age when perfectibility of mind and body by education and training seemed much more possible than they do to-day. " He had believed," Maria wrote of her father in her conclusion to his inimitable *Memoirs*, " that if rational creatures could be made clearly to see and understand that virtue will render them happy, and vice render them miserable, either in this world or the next, they would afterwards in consequence of this conviction follow virtue and avoid vice."

It was a time when it was claimed that " any character from the best to the worst may (by education) be given to the community " or to any individual, and it seemed scarcely less feasible that the human frame could undergo similar transformations. As a child Maria was thought rather small for her age, so an ingenious contrivance of ropes and pulleys was invented by which she was hanged every morning in the hopes of making her taller ; to no avail, it seems, for she was never anything but tiny. Thomas Day himself attempted to cure his knock-knees by the use of boards. " I have seen him," says Edgeworth, " stand between two boards which reached from the ground higher than his knees : these boards were adjusted with screws, so as barely to permit him to bend his knees, and to rise up and sit down. By these means M. Huise proposed to force

Mr. Day's knees outwards ; but his screwing was in vain. He succeeded in torturing his patient ; but original formation and inveterate habit resisted all his efforts at personal improvement. I could not help pitying my philosophic friend pent up in durance vile for hours together, with his feet in the stocks, a book in his hand and contempt in his heart."

Such people naturally adopted a stern attitude to literature. If the human frame was to be manipulated by stocks, human nature could be moulded by education, and literature was the right arm of education. The Industrial Revolution was getting under way, only barbers and dancing masters wore powdered wigs and the novel was falling into the hands of the pedagogue. The ease and safety of travel were now such that all journeys were robbed of adventure, men were making ascents in balloons, speeches were made in which it was declared that mankind was witnessing but the dawn of science, and there was a simple faith, by people like Bentham and Adam Smith, in the orderly and mechanical progress of civilisation ; and it was hard to believe that human nature was not making progress at just the same rate. Edgeworth, who was the friend of Erasmus Darwin, Wedgwood, James Watt, Herschel and Humphrey Davy, surveyed the mysteries of the human psyche and found that they were mysteries no longer. Two and two make four in experimental science, therefore two and two make four in the study of human personality.

To such a mind literature is only comprehensible in one way ; not as a criticism of life, not even as a faithful imitation of reality, still less as a form of art. Literature was a Warning. It was a Counterpoise to Corruption. It preached the greatest good of the greatest number and, unlike the revolutionary school of Bage, Holcroft, Godwin and Tom Paine with all their clatter about the rights of man, Edgeworth was of the opinion that literature was much more concerned with his duties.

It may be that Edgeworth's mother, who was a cripple and incapable of giving him the beating that even he occasionally deserved (he nearly killed his brother in a fit of temper), first showed him the power of the ascendant mind. Her only means of control over her son were those of reason and persuasion, and there is little doubt that Edgeworth was very considerably impressed by her success. When, in due course, he came to have a family of his own his code of discipline was based upon an appeal to reason, and since it was generally recognised that he was the chief repository of reason he gained, over the circle at Edgeworthstown, an ascendancy of mind that might well have embarrassed a less complacent man. " He inspired in my mind," Maria wrote shortly after his death, " a degree of hope and confidence essential in the first instance to the full exertion of the mental powers, and necessary to ensure perseverance in any occupation. Such, happily for me, was his power over my mind that no one thing I ever began to write was ever left unfinished."

Edgeworth's power over his daughter's mind amounted to far more than that, of course. His ideas became hers. In the preface which he contributed to Maria's *Tales of Fashionable Life* he stated : " It has therefore been my daughter's aim to promote, by all her writings, the progress of education from the cradle to the grave." From this there was no escape, except by death ; and Maria lived until she was eighty-two. She was well aware that she was not gifted with a bold, grand and dramatic style, and unlike Jane

2

Austen it grieved her that it should be so. Her manner was too Dutch, she said of herself, too minute. Had she been possessed of greater gifts she could have warned humanity against greater evils. But she found comfort. " The great virtues, the great vices excite strong enthusiasm, vehement horror, but after all it is not so necessary to warn the generality of mankind against these, either by precept or example, as against the lesser faults. . . . Show them the postern gates or little breaches in their citadel of virtue, and they fly to guard these."

Richard Lovell Edgeworth's influence over his daughter was not, as has sometimes been imagined, the superficial one of censor, nor is it true that he inserted sermons on utility into his daughter's lively novels ; those who have had access to the manuscripts say that his criticisms and interpolations made for improvement, they were sprightly and not at all didactic. The trouble lay deeper. Edgeworth's crime was not so much that he was a rather pompous and opinionated utilitarian but that he so conducted himself as to cause his daughter to love him uncritically and therefore adopt his precepts on literature and life unquestioningly. It was her honest opinion that Macbeth's speech, " Tomorrow and tomorrow and tomorrow," was a warning on the evils of procrastination.

It is much easier to write a caricature of Edgeworth than it is to do him the justice he deserves. By heaping up a list of his activities and opinions it is hard to avoid giving the impression of an assertive and dogmatic country gentle-man who thought he had the secret of the Universe in his pocket. There is truth in the picture, but a large family can be a testing ground for a man's character and we shall perhaps arrive at a truer assessment of his personality if we think of him as one of the most successful husbands and fathers on record. The more one reads of the great Edgeworth clan, their great love of life, their zest for knowledge, their simple-minded worship of the useful, the more Edgeworth emerges as a man strangely bigger than his ideas. He inspired an almost fanatic love in his wives and children and, after his death, a strong sense of his presence survived. " How *he* would have enjoyed it," is the thought that comes in the middle of any happy occasion after 1817 when, at the age of seventy-three, he died.

Within the family he reigned supreme but when he made his sallies into polite society there were those who thought him insufferable. It became noticeable to everyone (except perhaps to himself) that he was not receiving the deference to which family life had accustomed him. He could talk for ever. Nothing could stop him. Byron called him " a bore—the worst of bores—a boisterous bore." But then, Byron had probably been made the object of one of Edgeworth's most prized accomplishments, the ability " to draw a man out." One can just imagine this red-faced man from Ireland eyeing Byron, walking the length of the room to accost him and then subjecting him to a series of calculated questions. Nevertheless in Byron's diary (January 19, 1821, four years after Edgeworth's death) we find a more charitable verdict : " I thought Edgeworth a fine old fellow, of a clarety, elderly, red complexion, but active, brisk and endless . . . he bounced about and talked loud and long. . . . He seemed intelligent, vehement, vivacious and full of life. He bid fair for a hundred years. . . . The fact was everybody cared more about *her*. She was a nice little unassuming ' Jeanie-Deans-looking body ' as we Scotch say—and, if not handsome, certainly not ill-looking. Her

conversation was quiet as herself. One would never have
guessed that she could write *her name* ; whereas her father
talked, *not*, as if he could write nothing else, but as if nothing
else was worth writing."

1782 was an important year in Maria's life. She was
fifteen years of age and Mrs. Lataffiere's seminary for young
ladies at Derby and Mrs. Davis's establishment in Upper
Wimpole Street would know her no more—though she was
long remembered as an impromptu teller of stories on such
themes as the adventurer who disguised himself with a mask
of dried skin cut from a dead man's face. The important
circumstance of that year was not, however, leaving school
so much as the return to Ireland, together with the rest of
the family, that Mr. Edgeworth had decided upon.

It was not the first time Maria had been to Ireland. She
had been there as a child but what she remembered of her
experiences was as uncertain as a dream. Indeed, the bright
pictures that recurred to her might well have been dreams
for all their inconsequence ; she saw herself cutting out the
squares of a check sofa-cover and gaily trampling on a
number of hot-house frames and taking great pleasure in
the sound of breaking glass. They were memories from
another world, a far different world from either of her two
schools, for although she perfectly well remembered the joy
of cutting up the sofa-cover and smashing the garden frames,
she had no recollection of ever having been punished for
the damage she had caused.

It was appropriate for the return to this strange and happy
world that, although the month was June, snow should fall,
and it blanketed the roses in the garden of Edgeworthstown.
But almost immediately her father was insisting on taking

her out, on showing her the property and the improvements he intended to make. They made a tour of inspection on horseback together, and although she was a poor rider the presence of her father seemed to make all the difference to her horsemanship. He talked so delightfully, so entertainingly about the row of good slate houses that he would build for the peasants, of the measures that he would take against the evils of bailiffs and other middlemen that she almost forgot she was on horseback, and certainly forgot to be afraid.

It was clear that they were home to stay. At the age of thirty-eight Edgeworth was giving up the sights and dissipations of Clifton, Bath and London in order to devote himself to the improvement of his Irish property. The elegancies of the young ladies' seminaries had not prepared Maria for dealing with the peasant Irish which, as her father's chief assistant, she soon found herself called upon to do. It was work, this rent-collecting and estate management, that she was to carry out in one form or other for more than sixty years.

Only once between 1782 and 1802 did Maria leave Ireland, and that was for an extended stay in England, from autumn 1791 to autumn 1793, in company with the rest of the family. During those twenty years there were great changes at Edgeworthstown. Mr. Edgeworth had his new cottages built and found the best tenants for them—and by the best tenants he meant not those who paid the most rent but those who worked the hardest and improved the land. He reclaimed bog and mountain land, he designed wooden movable railways and small carriages to carry limestone and marl where it was most needed. Letters arrived from Dr. Darwin warning the family against the evils of drink :

" Farewell, my dear friend, God keep you from the whiskey—if He can," though Edgeworth was well known throughout the length and breadth of Ireland for his temperance. A new baby arrived every year and Edgeworth, as though impatient with the slow processes of nature, contemplated adopting a peasant child and educating him for a higher rank. Children died and even Mr. Day himself, after marrying a woman who showed him all the respect and adulation which he knew he deserved, fell in 1789 a victim to his own benevolence. He had noticed that horse-breaking was sometimes a vicious process and decided to train a horse by gentler means. But it took fright at a man winnowing corn and Mr. Day was thrown on his head never to speak again. Since 1782 the Edgeworths had seen but little of him, for he had been living first in Essex and then in Surrey, but the news cast a gloom over the family in Ireland.

Unlike most landowners Edgeworth dispensed with the services of bailiffs and middlemen who, by crooked dealings, frequently made more than their masters and oppressed the peasantry. He also abolished the feudal dues, the payment of duty fowls and the duty work, and insisted that all rents should be paid into his own hand. This meant that there was a great deal of business to carry out and, as was typical of the man, he saw to it that the whole family understood just what he was doing. It was part of their education. " Not only his wife but his children knew all his affairs," Maria wrote. " Whatever business he had to do was done in the midst of the family, usually in the common sitting-room, so that we were intimately acquainted not only with his general principles of conduct, but with the most minute details of their everyday application. I further enjoyed some peculiar advantages ; he wished to give me habits of business and allowed me during many years to assist him in copying his letters of business and receiving his rents."

She was gaining that knowledge of the difficulties and triumphs of ordinary life, and of Irish peasant life in particular, that was to be the backbone of her novels. Edgeworth himself had a great zest for the turns of Irish humour and the oddities of peasant character. It only needed a good government, he would say, for the creation of a great country ; for while the upper and middle classes were of very poor quality the peasants themselves, though cruel and ignorant, were good and simple raw material. Whenever he came home, perhaps from the magistrate's court or a trip to Dublin, he had some good story to tell—and he told it with the same enthusiasm with which he recited Shakespeare or Pope's translation of the *Iliad*. He had great talent for imitating the Irish, he knew just how to hit off their happy confidence, their shrewd wit and their pathos. These anecdotes Maria made a point of recording, and she sighed that she could not set down the inflexions and quick turns of her father's speech.

When she was not acting as her father's bailiff and secretary Maria was helping to educate her young brothers and sisters. Henry, born in 1782, was her special charge. For the general entertainment of the younger members of the family she would write what she called " wee, wee stories " on a slate. They were then read out, discussed and, if approved, copied out in ink. No doubt it was a practice that was going on in country houses throughout the length and breadth of Great Britain. Those large, enthusiastic families provided ideal breeding grounds for the young novelist. She—it was inevitably she—had a ready-made audience at her mercy and creative writing came to her as naturally as a charade.

It was not, as it so frequently is to-day, an act of faith directed towards an unknown, unpredictable and sometimes alien public. Most of these stories and novels written for a particular family or group of friends did not, of course, get so far as the printer's press. For many, as in the case of Maria Edgeworth's tales for children, publication was almost irrelevant. The approval that she set most store by, that of her father to whom a plan was submitted before each story was elaborated, and that of her brothers and sisters, had already been gained. And, just as her father conducted his business in the common living-room with the life of the family going on all around, so did Maria write her stories and later her novels. In just the same way did Jane Austen go to work. The novels were the expression of a class and, above all, of the family within that class, in a way that was so soon to pass away. The Brontë sisters, for example, never quite knew what the other was doing, and Charlotte actually came across Emily's poems by accident. But for years Jane Austen was sustained by the audience that her family provided ; her novels were family entertainments with private jokes into which the public, years after they were originally conceived, were generously admitted. For Maria Edgeworth, as for Jane Austen, writing was never a process that went on in solitude, there was no sense of division between her and her prospective readers, and she never feared that she might be talking to an empty room.

In Maria's tales for children we meet the first living and breathing children in English literature since Shakespeare. What kind of stories were they ? In spite of Dr. Johnson the eighteenth century had set its face against fairy stories. " Babies do not like," he said, " to hear stories about babies like themselves ; they require to have their imaginations

raised by tales of giants and fairies, and castles and enchant-
ments." But such delights were frowned upon by those
who took most interest in the welfare of children. Rousseau,
quite as much as Locke, considered that the useful had sufficient magic of its own and the lesser, trivial magic of Charles
Perrault (the biographer of Cinderella, Red Riding Hood,
the Sleeping Beauty, Puss in Boots and how many others)
and of the Arabian Nights Entertainments, was expected
to wither at the break of day. It is a solemn thought, for
example, that Madame de Genlis could compress her lips
and say that although she had read many fairy tales and
stories from the Arabian Nights she had quite failed to find
any moral tendency in them ; what, we may wonder,
would she have said if she had read the Arabian Nights in
Burton's unexpurgated translation ? Edgeworth, however,
agreed with her. He had enough common sense to und r-
stand the delight with which children heard of flying h rses
and magic mirrors—he had read the Arabian Nights aloud
to the children of Edgeworthstown—" But is this a reason
why they should be indulged in reading them ? It may be
said that a little experience in life would soon convince them
that fairies, giants and enchanters are not to be met with in
the world. But why should the mind be filled with fantastic
visions instead of useful knowledge ? "

A moral story, we might reply, is just as much a fantastic
vision as anything in the Arabian Nights. To a child a good
moral, if presented in the right way, is every bit as satisfying
as a cloak of invisibility and just as much of a delusion.
None of these writers of moral stories, from the great
Marmontel who wrote for grown-ups to Armand Berquin
who was the Marmontel of the nursery, could afford to
dispense with the magic of moral rectitude. Thomas Day's

Sandford and Merton is, as every child of the time knew, as full of magic as a witch's cauldron. Take, for example, the story of the Good-Natured Boy. He is going to a certain village and carrying a basket of provisions. But on the way he meets a starving dog, an afflicted horse, a crippled sailor, and a blind man who is standing in the middle of a pond in imminent danger of drowning. The boy feeds the dog and the crippled sailor from his store of provisions, brings grass to the afflicted horse and rescues the blind man from his pond.

There are now a number of possibilities. Most children of intelligence would tell us that the boy would now get into trouble for dawdling and receive a spanking for giving away what did not belong to him. But in the Thomas Day world of moralistic magic events turn out in a very different way. The boy is lost in a wood—it is a magic wood but Mr. Day does not tell us this—and having given away all his food he is very hungry. It is at this point that the clockwork having been wound up by so many good deeds begins to whirr. The dog runs up with a handkerchief in his mouth. On opening the handkerchief the boy discovers that it contains sandwiches. (How Mr. Day must have been puzzled to think how a dog could carry sandwiches in a *nice* way !) And then the horse arrives to carry the boy safely out of the wood. But all danger is not yet past. The boy is set upon by two robbers. He is, of course, rescued by the blind man and the cripple who together make a fearsome spectacle. The cripple is riding on the blind man's shoulders. The robbers are frightened off by the arrival of this giant and so the boy receives his reward, his mathematically calculated reward, for all his good deeds.

Maria was infinitely Day's superior not only in the water-colour freshness of her children but in her ability to exploit moral magic to its full. In *The Parent's Assistant* (1796) there is a characteristic story called *Waste Not, Want Not*. The original idea for this story might have been within Day's powers but the ruthless, the relentless march of catastrophe resulting from a fatal flaw of character would have been quite beyond him. A Bristol merchant has invited two of his nephews to stay with him so that he can decide which of them he will adopt. These two boys, Ben and Hal, are contrasts dear to the heart of all moralists—we find their prototypes in Maria's teachers, in Marmontel, in Berquin, in Madame de Genlis. Ben is prudent and careful. Hal is improvident and selfish. The first test comes when they are each given a parcel to untie. Hal, the improvident, cuts the cord " precipitately in sundry places," but Ben, knowing that it is a magic piece of string, carefully unties his and places it in his pocket. We say that it is a magic piece of string because nothing else is sufficient to explain their uncle's next action, that of presenting each of the boys with a top. Ben, of course, has his " excellent piece of whipcord." Hal takes the string off his hat. From now on the course of events is as inexorable as in a Greek tragedy. Little Patty, their girl cousin, trips over Hal's discarded loop of whipcord and falls down the stairs. She sprains her ankle and Ben, to amuse her as she lies upon her sick bed, draws out his length of whipcord to play at cat's cradle. The uncle smiles indulgently and makes a remark which sounds ironical but which is most certainly not : " I shall not think you one bit less manly because I see you playing at cat's-cradle with a little child of six years old."

There is now to be an archery contest. On the way to the meeting Hal's hat is blown off by the wind (we remember the wrongful purpose to which he had put his hat-string) and in chasing it he falls into the mud and ruins his beautiful green and white uniform. His final humiliation is yet to come. It is a rule of the contest that participants can only use one bow. When Hall goes to shoot his arrow his bowstring snaps and he has to retire from the contest. Curiously enough, the same misfortune happens to Ben. He is seen, however, drawing something from his pocket which brings a cry from Hal's lips, a cry from the darkness of the human predicament : " The eternal whipcord, I declare." We can only echo that cry.

There is a great deal more to these stories, however, than can be conveyed by any summary. They have more than the magic of rectitude. They have the charm of brightly painted pictures. The Bristol streets and shops glitter in the morning sunshine and in the cathedral a robin hops and sings. Maria knew just the touch that will draw the child's attention, the green and white uniform, the coloured jars in a chemist's window (in *The Purple Jar*), all the bright, enticing joy of the simple objects of the material world. We are happy to think of the little girl who shared her bread and milk with a pig, or the " little breathless girl " who ran back to thank Simple Susan for her gift of flowers, crying, " Kiss me quick, for I shall be left behind."

But there is a rebel in this world of common sense. Her name is Rosamond. She is cheerful, generous, impetuous and entirely delightful. Given the choice of a new pair of shoes and the purple jar in the chemist's window she chooses the purple jar. And here she is in a story called *The Birthday Present*.

> " Dear mother ! don't you remember that it's the 22nd of December ? And her birthday is the day after tomorrow, don't you recollect now ? But you never remember abou

birthdays, mamma ; that was just what I was thinking of, that you never remember my sister Laura's birthday, or—or—or *mine*, mamma."

"What do you mean my dear ? I remember your birthday perfectly well."

"Indeed, but you never keep it though."

"What do you mean by keeping your birthday ? "

"Oh, mamma, you know very well—as Bell's birthday is kept. In the first place there is a great dinner."

"And can Bell eat more upon her birthday than upon any other day ? "

"No : nor should I mind about the dinner, except the mince-pies. But Bell has many nice things : I don't mean nice eatable things ; but nice new playthings given to her always on her birthday ; and everybody drinks her health, and she's so happy ! "

"But stay Rosamond, how you jumble things together ! Is it everybody's drinking her health that makes her so happy, or the new playthings, or the nice mince-pies ? I can easily believe that she is happy whilst she is eating a mince-pie, or whilst she is playing ; but how does everybody's drinking her health at dinner make her happy ? "

Rosamond paused and then said that she did not know.

"But," added she, " the *nice new* playthings, mother ! "

And Rosamond spends her half-guinea on making a basket for Bell with some filigree paper, a basket that is so fragile that it is easily broken. Rosamond's sister Laura (she is the prudent one) gives her half-guinea to a poor girl. No one appreciates this generosity more than Rosamond who sees how silly she had been herself in thinking that birthdays were days of special celebration, and how absurd it was to spend money on useless gifts. She takes the quiet determination to be more sensible and prudent in future. Poor Rosamond does this in story after story, but she never quite succeeds in taming her uncalculating love of life.

It is important to remember that whereas Jane Austen's

approach to writing was satirical Maria Edgeworth's was markedly educational. The very first literary task she ever undertook was the translation of Madame de Genlis's moral story for children, *Adèle et Théodore*. Mr. Edgeworth sat up until the early hours working at the correction, but even so the work was never published because it was anticipated by the appearance of another, and probably better, translation. Mr. Thomas Day, who was then still alive, had a horror of female authorship and when he learned that Maria's translation was not after all to be published he wrote a letter of congratulation on so narrow an escape from so great an evil. Mr. Edgeworth ventured to disagree. Under certain circumstances, where the work was of a strongly moral and useful nature, there was a lot to be said for the females. His reply, we may well imagine, was read aloud to the family before its despatch, and nearly ten years later, in 1795, Maria based her *Letters for Literary Ladies* upon her memories of Mr. Day's eloquence and her father's reasoned reply. Day was already dead but even so Maria and her father had the obscure feeling that they had sinned against his memory by allowing such a publication to go forward. The work gained an immediate reputation for Maria. Compared with Mary Wollstonecraft's *Vindication of the Rights of Women* this plea for reform in women's education is a very tepid affair and is of small interest but for the picture it gives of the ideal young lady as we later meet her in the pages of Jane Austen and of Maria herself. " The imagination of the young lady must not be raised above the taste for necessary occupations, or the numerous small but trifling pleasures of domestic life ; her mind must be enlarged, yet the delicacy of her manners must be preserved, her knowledge must be various, and her powers of reasoning unawed by authority ;

yet she must habitually feel that nice sense of propriety which is at once the guard and the charm of every feminine virtue." This is Belinda, just as it is Elizabeth Bennet. But the suggestion that the ideal qualities for a woman are modesty, timidity and demureness aroused the greatest indignation in Mary Wollstonecraft, an indignation that was not calmed by Maria's startling suggestion that governesses should receive £300 a year.

It was the writer's obvious duty to warn the reader of the evils that would result when, as in *Northanger Abbey*, the imagination is raised "above the taste for necessary occupations," and Maria's apparent coldness to this novel was possibly due to her belief that Catherine was not sufficiently punished for her absurdities. A heightened imagination was not the only evil against which the young lady requires warning, however. Different warnings are required at different ages, and warnings suitable for boys are not suitable for girls. And, much as we should like to believe it, young men and young women are not beyond reproach. They must, in due measure, receive the admonishments they failed to receive in childhood. A writer's ambition, it followed, should be to cover the life-span of an ordinary human being with detailed warnings. It was rather like papering a room with postage stamps.

The Parent's Assistant, *Moral Tales* and *Popular Tales* were written by Maria to exemplify (Mr. Edgeworth's word) the principles set out in *Practical Education* (1798), and the *Tales of Fashionable Life* which Maria published between 1809 and 1812 were later intended to illustrate the ideas set out in *Professional Education* (1808). *Practical Education*, which Edgeworth wrote in collaboration with his wife Honora and Maria, is an important book in educational history ;

Professional Education (since it seemed to suggest that parents should choose their sons' professions at birth) is a misguided one. But good or bad, was there ever a writer as handicapped as Maria was? There seemed to be a silent assumption that the really important work had been done in *Practical Education* and *Professional Education*. Maria's stories were merely in elaboration. With these factors in mind her achievement is all the more remarkable. Her stories are alive in spite of the propaganda.

Considerations other than literary ones give interest to these early stories. When Maria accompanied her father to Paris during the experimental peace of 1802 she had the pleasure of meeting Madame d'Ouditot who, as a child, had inspired Rousseau with the idea for Julie. Maria was delighted with her. "Julie is now 72 years of age, a thin woman in a little black bonnet : she appeared to me shockingly ugly . . . but no sooner did I hear her speak than I began to like her. . . . She seems as gay and open-hearted as a girl of fifteen. . . . She is possessed of that art which Lord Kames said he would prefer to the finest gift of the fairies—the art of seizing the best side of every object. . . . Even during the horrors of the Revolution, if she met with a flower, a butterfly, an agreeable smell, a pretty colour, she would turn her attention to these and for the moment suspend her sense of misery, not from frivolity, but from real philosophy."

This description can well be applied to Maria herself. There had been disturbances in Ireland for many years and the class to which Maria belonged lived in fear of a general rising. " All that I crave," Maria wrote to her favourite aunt Ruxton, " for my own part is, that if I am to have my throat cut, it may not be by a man with his face blackened with charcoal." This was the period during which she was writing her children's stories and collecting anecdotes for the study of Irish humour which she and her father were later to publish under the title of *An Essay on Irish Bulls*. The Defenders, as the rebels called themselves, disguised their voices and faces by sticking pieces of broken tobacco pipe at the corner of their mouths, and attacked country houses such as Edgeworthstown for ammunition. Then, in 1798, the French succeeded in landing an expeditionary force in Ireland, the Defenders roamed the countryside —and Mr. Edgeworth, for the fourth and last time, got married! While Maria was writing anxious letters to Dublin, anxious lest the lilacs and laburnums in the garden should have finished flowering before the arrival of the new mistress of the household, he was driving his wife homewards, passing a cart on which the rebels had hanged a man.

Mr. Edgeworth, enjoying himself immensely, set about organising a troop of yeomanry as soon as he arrived at Edgeworthstown. Maria says that all the men seemed very attached to him—" but alas! by some strange negligence their arms have not arrived from Dublin." A body of rebels armed with pikes were reported within a few miles of the house and it became necessary for the family to leave. They were offered the protection of two officers and six dragoons who were escorting an ammunition cart from Mullingar to Longford, but for some reason Mr. Edgeworth declined. Had he accepted the history of English literature might well have been different. Half an hour after the departure of the ammunition cart there was a sound like a clap of thunder. The ammunition cart had taken fire and exploded. When, an hour or two afterwards, the family made its way towards the comparative security of Longford they passed the sight of the catastrophe and averted their eyes.

After an interval of four days, during which time Mr. Edgeworth was accused of being a spy for the French and knocked on the head with a brickbat, they returned home once more and were greeted by the cats who, Maria said, " crowded round Kitty with congratulatory faces, crawling up her gown, insisting on caressing and being caressed." And, in next to no time—or so it seemed—Mr. Edgeworth had transformed the room over his study into a little theatre and it was announced to Maria that they were going to write a comedy, and the names of the chief characters were going to be Mrs. Fangle, Sir Mordant Idem, Count Babel-hausen and Heliodorus.

The French invasion, the explosion of the ammunition cart, the hostile demonstration of the mob at Longford, had been little more than ripples on the calm surface of the life of this large, self-contained and, one is tempted to say, self-satisfied family. The bright conversation recommenced in the library and Maria worked away on the little writing table (the contraptions and gadgets may be imagined) that her father had made for her, quite undisturbed by the noise of the family from whom she received no concessions as a writer and from whom she expected none. " She wrote on folio sheets of paper," we learn from her stepmother, " which she sewed together in chapters. To facilitate the calculation of the MS. for printing, and to secure each page containing nearly the same amount of writing, she used to prick the margin of her paper at equal distances, and her father made a little machine set with points by which she could pierce several sheets at once."

Mr. Edgeworth had long noticed that society was divided

up into classes ; it therefore followed that the moral instruction for different classes should proceed on different
lines. The faults of the genteel were not the faults of
the poorer classes. The genteel were afflicted with bad
governesses, the evil influence of servants, uncalculating
generosity and foolish enthusiasm ; humbler folk were given
to laziness, dishonesty and lack of thrift. Burke had calculated that there were about 80,000 readers in Great Britain
and Mr. Edgeworth made the further calculation that
10,000 of these belonged to the nobility, the clergy or
gentlemen of the learned professions. The *Moral Tales* were
therefore slanted to the younger members of these upper
classes, young people too old for *The Parent's Assistant* ; and
Popular Tales represents a bold attempt to corner the youth
of less elegant society.

There is nothing to set beside the primrose freshness of
Simple Susan, but there are things good enough. Mr. Edgeworth must have been particularly gratified by *The Good
French Governess* who is a character to compare with the
formidable Madame de Genlis herself. From this story alone
it would be possible to reconstruct the main lines of *Practical
Education* : the children do not play with dolls, they have
such rational toys as bricks for building, ruler and pencil for
making architectural drawings and, if we are to place reliance
upon Dr. Darwin's definition, they are anything but fools.
" A fool, Edgeworth," the Doctor said, " is a man who
never conducted an experiment in his life." Under the
influence of the Good French Governess the children make
many experiments. *Angelina* is a good story in its own
right. But the best of the *Moral Tales* is undoubtedly *Forester*.
Here, very thinly disguised, is none other than the great Mr.
Thomas Day himself. He refuses to dress according to his

station in life, he despises dancing and girls, and runs away from his kind guardian to take a job as a gardener. Henry, the guardian's son, is on the other hand a complete Edgeworth boy. He never acts precipitately and bears himself like a man of forty. Furthermore he has the world of science at his fingertips. He is able to save the life of a friend's canary because he has read Falconer's treatise on poisons. The climax of the story is reached when Forester is falsely accused of stealing a banknote and Henry is able to establish his innocence by keen observation, close reasoning and a knowledge of the effects of vitriolic acid. Forester, or Thomas Day if we like, has to admit that he has behaved very foolishly. He learns to dance. The story gives some measure of the distance that Mr. Edgeworth had travelled since his early enthusiasm for Rousseau. It is the story of civilisation triumphant.

Maria's juvenile stories enjoyed extraordinary popularity. The little girl who ran up to Maria in the middle of a crowded room and panted out, "I like Simple Susan best," before, overcome with confusion, running to hide, had made a perfectly good answer to Dr. Johnson's pronouncement in favour of ogres and fairies. Children liked the tales of magic *and* the tales of improvement (provided Maria wrote them) because every word she wrote was illuminated with a love and understanding of the child mind. "How is it," she was asked, "that you know so much about children?" "I don't know," she said mildly, "I lie down and let them crawl over me."

The days of magic were over and Roger Bacon, who had once been thought of as a wizard, was now the inventor of gunpowder and the camera obscura, the balloon was the new Pegasus, science had succeeded to poetry. But the children who know all this were real children, living in real houses, in real and identifiable parts of the countryside. " At the foot of a steep, slippery white hill near Dunstable," one of the stories begins. " In a retired hamlet on the borders of Wales, between Oswestry and Shrewsbury——"; " In the pleasant vale of Ashton——"; " In the neighbourhood of a seaport in the West of England——"; " It was Sunday morning, and a fine day in autumn, the bells of Hereford rang, and all the world, smartly dressed, was flocking to church."

Children can be the most logical and realistic of creatures and these stories satisfied that part of the imagination which craved for the possible and the actual. " Tell Miss Edgeworth I do really think that Rosamond was foolish not to choose the shoes, but her Mama made her go without them very long. I would not have made her go barefoot more than a week," said one little boy aged four to his mother. Another, aged nine, " Really that is a very useful as well as an entertaining book. I have learned a great many things from it that I did not know before." They were picking up elementary science, they were taken on journeys to India, to China and America, they made clocks, went up in balloons and looked at the moon through Mr. Herschel's telescope.

The clear-cut character contrasts were satisfying to the child's mind : the spoilt child and the prudent child, the impetuous Rosamond and the more thoughtful Laura, the enthusiastic Helen and the wiser Emma, and yet even the good are differentiated from each other so that there is no confusing Rosamond with Helen, and Laura with Emma. There was the enlivenment of such touches as the Irish labourer who, on being called a quarrelsome man, offered to fight anyone who dared repeat such a libel : " I'd fight

him here in your honour's presence, if he'd only come out
this minute and meet me like a man." Or Mlle. Panache
the French governess who was really a milliner and gave
herself away by putting seventeen pins in her mouth.
" *Qu'avez vous donc ! Ce n'est rien ! Ah, si vous aviez vu
Mlle. Alexandre !* Ah, dat would frighten you indeed !
Many de time I see her put one, tirty, forty, fifty—ay, one
hundred, two hundred—in her mouth and she all de time
laugh, talk, eat, drink, sleep wid dem, and no harm, *non
obstant*, never happen Mlle. Alexandre."

Many of these stories were based upon members of the
Edgeworth household and upon the children of the neighbourhood. There seems to have been some agreement about
the identity of Rosamond.

On his death-bed Richard Lovell Edgeworth called his
family around him. " I have called you to listen to something of consequence I am saying to Maria. When I die,
you, Maria, will be left in excellent circumstances. You
will be rich. You have many brothers and sisters and friends,
who may each in their turn have claims upon you. You
will want to give away your fortune, first to one, then to
another—you will give the same sum twice over and forget
that you have given it, and wonder you have it not still."

On her knees she promised to be good (she was then over
fifty years of age.) He proceeded. " You are the only one
of my children of whom I have anything to beg. My eldest
son is wise and economic. My daughter Fanny is prudence
itself. My wife—but anything more I could say would only
weaken the impression."

And, ten years later, we find Maria writing to her Aunt
Ruxton to tell her of the *great progress* she was resolved to
make.

She thinks, smiles and adds a message that everyone in the family would understand immediately—*Rosamond at sixty*.

But if Rosamond was Maria who are we to identify with the astonishing little boy of *Early Lessons* ?

> When his father or mother said to him, " Frank, shut the door," he ran directly and shut the door. When they said to him, " Frank, do not touch that knife," he took his hands away from the knife, and did not touch it. He was an obedient little boy.

Frank lingers in the memory. He dominated the nursery tale for fifty years. Then Hawthorne published his *Tanglewood Tales* and, in 1865 with the coming of Alice, fantasy burst about little Frank's head. He was never so good after that.

Had Maria Edgeworth been blown up with the ammunition cart in 1798 we should not have known what we had lost. *Castle Rackrent* (1800) is not, perhaps, the masterpiece that it has been claimed. It is a novel only if a prose narrative of something under 30,000 words in length can be called a novel ; but it is the most alive piece of sustained writing that Maria was to achieve and, since it launched her into the writing of her Irish stories, it is the most influential narrative prose between the death of Smollett and the publication of *Waverley*. Through Scott, Maria's Irish stories have been one of the fountheads of inspiration for European novelists. His aim, Scott wrote in the postscript to *Waverley*, had been " in some distant degree to emulate the admirable Irish portraits drawn by Miss Edgeworth." If we are to believe a letter which appeared in the London *Daily News* on September 7, 1883, signed by " One who knew Turgenev," Maria was a direct stimulus to that fine artist also. He is reported to have stated that he was " an unconscious disciple of Miss Edgeworth in setting out on his literary career " and but for the squires of Longford he might not have thought of describing those of Russia. *Castle Rackrent* is the great ancestor of the regional novel.

Never had Maria so enjoyed herself. The year being 1798 her father was too much occupied with outside matters to have much time for his daughter's literary endeavours. He had no hand in *Castle Rackrent*. Yet Maria never seemed to be able to dispense with the active encouragement of some-one or other. In this case it was her beloved Aunt Ruxton and under her quiet influence all Maria's peasant knowledge and Irish lore came welling up.

When she had returned to Ireland in 1782 she had been much struck by the conversation and manners of a peasant retainer. The man remained in her memory and, except for the fact that he is made older so that he can span two gen-erations of the Rackrent family, this is Thady, the narrator of *Castle Rackrent*. Following one of the fashions of the time the book is an edited manuscript which the editor ventures to place before the public as illustrating customs and manners which were fast passing away. Maria wrote the book when she was thirty but it is a book written out of the innocence of heart, the enthusiasm for fresh scenes and fresh faces, of fifteen ; it is a debt paid by the mature authoress of *Moral Tales* to the reserved child who came home to find snow on the roses of Edgeworthstown.

Thady stands before us. " I wear a long greatcoat, winter and summer, which is very handy, as I never put my arms into the sleeves ; they are as good as new, though come Holantide next I've had it these seven years ; it holds on by a single button round my neck, cloak fashion." He has heard from his grandfather of the times when old Sir Patrick ruled over Castle Rackrent, and he was a man who could sit out the best man in Ireland, let alone the three kingdoms itself. From one year's end to another there were so many guests in his house that Sir Patrick had the chicken house fitted up to take the overflow. He was said to be the inventor of raspberry whisky but it was not even for that we find Thady revering his memory, though he had never seen him ; it was because the old gentleman lived well, threw his money away and drank himself to death. " The whole country," said Thady, " rang with his praises. Happy the man who could but get a sight of the hearse ! But who'd have thought it ? Just as all was going on right, through his own town they were passing, when the body was seized for debt."

Thady's great concern is always for the honour of the family, but he has his own notions of the trappings of honour ; it had a great deal to do with display and openness of heart. " God bless him ! He valued a guinea as little as any man : money to him was no more than dirt." Sir Murtagh, who succeeded Sir Patrick, was afflicted by a parsimonious wife, but found consolation in a passion for litigation. " He used to boast that he had a lawsuit for every letter in the alphabet. . . . Out of forty-nine suits which he had, he never lost one but seventeen." But he made the mistake of digging up a fairy mount and things never prospered with him after that. He broke a blood vessel in a fit of anger with his lady, died, was buried and succeeded by the swaggering, fighting Sir Kit. Sir Kit was an absentee landlord. " He had the spirit of a prince and lived away to the honour of his country abroad." But when he came to the end of his money he married a wealthy

Jewess, brought her home to Castle Rackrent, tormented her with pork sausages and bacon and shut her up in her room for seven years because she would not hand over a diamond cross. On the rumour of her death three ladies presented themselves as candidates for his second wife. Sir Kit fought duels with the ladies' brothers. The first he shot, but the second had a wooden leg which stuck fast in a new-ploughed field and Sir Kit " with great candour fired his pistol over his head." The third brother shot Sir Kit and the new Sir Condy Rackrent hastened over from England. Sir Condy is treated at greater length than the others for on his head falls the accumulated doom of the Rackrent generations.

Maria had a taste for the preposterous and, like many another writer, she was at her best when sailing very close to caricature. It was a vein that Mr. Edgeworth did not appreciate. When Lady Morgan's *O'Donnell* was being read to the family he complained that the scene of M'Rory's appearance in the billiard room was quite improbable. " Never mind the improbability," Maria exclaimed, " let us go on with the story." Yet, although she was prepared to accept the improbable (provided it was amusing) in other people's stories, just as she and her father accepted the Arabian Nights and other tales of magic so long as they were not expected to write them or approve of them, she was always more critical of her own compositions. She was concerned, for example, lest *Castle Rackrent* should be thought incredible and therefore unintelligible to the English reader. Her fears were, of course, groundless. The book achieved tremendous success, and since it was published anonymously one gentleman went so far as to copy out a few pages, with some erasures and alterations of his own, which he then presented as the original manuscript and himself as the author.

Anything in the text which might appear particularly unusual, as for example Sir Kit's shutting up his wife for seven years, is carefully documented and the " history of the celebrated Lady Cathcart's conjugal imprisonment " quoted in a long footnote. In later novels Maria was to content herself with an asterisk in the text and the single word " Fact " at the bottom of the page. This stress between what Maria knew not only to be possible but true and what she felt her readers to be capable of believing led, later on, to a sober under-writing of her material, a leaving out of a great deal of interesting material (in *Ormond*, for example) and an interesting declaration that " a perfectly true character absolutely taken as facsimile from real life would not be interesting in a fiction, might not be believed and could not be useful."

Castle Rackrent is such a joy to read because it was written in a spirit of unreflecting pleasure and of identification with Old Thady the narrator. " I could not write dialogues at all," Maria said, " without being at the time fully impressed with the characters, imagining myself each speaker." Sir Patrick, Sir Condy and Sir Kit do not exist in their own right. They exist in the mind of Thady himself, in the medium of his misplaced sense of family honour, his lack of surprise at what would otherwise seem incredible, his peasant knack for placing the emphasis just a little differently from the sophisticated. If Thady is authentic then the people Thady talks about share his authenticity. " If I could," wrote Scott to James Ballantyne, " but hit Miss Edgeworth's wonderful power of vivifying all her persons and making them live as *being* in your mind, I should not be afraid.'

We no more doubt the existence of the Rackrent family
than Thady does himself. This is a doubt that can all the
more easily creep in when the author looks at his material
simply and directly from his own point of view. " Give a
man a mask and he will speak the truth," said Wilde. Thady
is Maria's mask. Once in position the rest follows with very
little contrivance.

One of the great triumphs of the story is Attorney Quirk,
the go-getting, unscrupulous lawyer son of Old Thady
himself. The stature of the rascal is not immediately
apparent for he is sketched with the very lightest of touches.
Thady cannot say out and out that his son is the villain
who, next to the Rackrents themselves, was chiefly respons-
ible for their downfall. " I wash my hands of his doings,"
says Thady, and that is as far as he will go. It is Thady's
very restraint that gives the attorney his actuality. Very
soberly Thady relates how his son, by guile rather than by
ability, gained the agency of the Rackrent estates during the
absenteeship of Sir Kit. He has the three-dimensional
solidity of a figure illuminated from two sides. More is
left to the imagination than is specified in Thady's chronicle
of his son's scheming, only just enough to explain the
catastrophe. Had the attorney been any other than Thady's
son, had Thady called him a villain every time he appeared
in the story, he would have lost the benefit of that second
illumination which holds a character more firmly in what
the imagination takes to be the real world than any amount
of complex characterisation. " When you depict sad or
unlucky people," said Chekov, " and you want to touch
your readers' hearts, try to be cold—it gives their grief a
background against which it stands out in greater relief."
At the beginning of the story the attorney is nobody ; at

the end he is the proud occupier of Castle Rackrent and the dispossessed owner lies dying in the lodge. What Chekov said about grief is also true of the other emotions. The attorney is a villain but Thady's reluctance to admit the fact provides just that background to set him off with a reality of which Scott was so soon to find the secret.

It is typical of the improvident Sir Condy that he marries for neither money nor love, but simply because her father forbade the match and she was so desperately in love with him. When he arrives home with his bride there are panes of glass missing from the windows and the wind whistles down the dusty corridors. It is impossible to drive up to the front door because the great piers had tumbled down and the approach was blocked with ruins. His real affections had fallen upon Judy M'Quirk, a niece of Old Thady. In fact, Condy was so torn between Judy and the woman who became his wife that he could only settle the question by the toss of a coin. The bills and threatening letters flow in, a couple of writs are issued and the sheriff lets it be known that he will do his duty if it was against the first man in the country, or even his own brother, let alone against one who had voted against him at the last election as Sir Condy had done. Lady Rackrent returns to her family and then, with the doors clapping and the rain coming in through the roof, Sir Condy sits down with a mountain of bills to settle his affairs.

The firmness with which Maria sustains the comic spirit of *Castle Rackrent* is her greatest artistic achievement. The tone of ironic detachment never wavers (as it sometimes does waver in *Belinda* and *The Absentee*) because no sooner does Thady build up a scene of desolation and hopelessness than he immediately " kills " it with a stroke of farce.

"Thady," Sir Condy said, "I've a great fancy to see my own funeral afore I die." What might have been pathos turns out to be comedy. Lying under the bedclothes and greatcoats Sir Condy is given an Irish "wake." The room is thronged with men, women and children, all smoking, talking and laughing. After a while he thought he would be stifled with the weight of clothes upon him, sat up and sent for some whisky from a shebeen-house ("where they very civilly let him have it upon credit") and there was merrymaking all night.

After the mock funeral Judy M'Quirk walks in—but a very much changed Judy. She has been married for a couple of years and is now a widow. Her looks are gone.

"How's this Judy?" says Sir Condy. "I take it a little amiss of you that you were not at my wake last night."

"Ah, don't be being jealous of that," says she, "I didn't hear a sentence of your honour's wake till it was all over, or it would have gone hard with me but I would have been at it, sure; but I was forced to go ten miles up the country three days ago to a wedding of a relation of my own's, and didn't get home till after the wake was over. But," says she, "it won't be so, I hope, the next time, please your honour."

This is the first time that Judy appears in the story in person. Previously we have only heard of her as a beautiful girl as fond of Sir Condy as he is of her. When she does arrive it is with the solidity of the unexpected. No reconciliation here, no gathering of belated rosebuds. Judy has suffered greatly and sees that Sir Condy is finished and that her best chance for advancement is through marrying the attorney. Sir Condy dies as a result of a bet that he could not drink the contents of a great horn without stopping ; " But," says Thady in the same breath, almost as though it were the most important feature of the whole incident, " he had but a very poor funeral after all."

No one had been writing like this since the death of Smollett.

1802 was the year of peace. In the very first mail packet to Calais there were no less than sixty-three English ladies burning for a glimpse of the latest Paris fashions and all the latest novelties, of which the First Consul was the most important. At a time when photography was yet to be invented no reliable likeness of Napoleon had found its way to London, and there was a great deal of speculation and argument about the personal appearance of the new dictator. It was the year, also, when the *Essay on Irish Bulls* was published. This was by far the happiest result of Edgeworth's collaboration with his daughter. Maria said that it was quite impossible to recollect which of the thoughts were originally his and which was hers. It is worth recording that this essay on Irishisms was purchased by the Secretary to the Irish Agricultural Society under the misapprehension that it was a treatise on the improvement of Irish cattle.

But the news from Paris was too exciting to be resisted. All the intellect and wit of Europe had gathered in the City of Light and Edgeworth felt that his absence might be remarked. In the middle of September, therefore, together with Mrs. Edgeworth, Maria and Charlotte, one of his other daughters, he set off to gratify his French friends and revive memories of what people were already regarding as the " good old days." They travelled by way of Leicester and London ; at Leicester an interesting experience befell them.

The Edgeworths were presented to a local authoress, a

certain Miss Watts who had been much admired for her translation of Tasso and had recently published a volume of poems. Miss Watts, who was tall and fair, young and quite pretty, took Mrs. Edgeworth for the celebrated authoress. She " darted forward with arms, long thin arms, outstretched to their utmost swing, ' OH, WHAT AN HONOUR THIS IS ! ' each word and syllable rising in tone till the last reached a scream. Instead of embracing my mother," Maria writes, " as her first action threatened, she started back to the farthest end of the room, which was not light enough to show her attitude distinctly, but it seemed to be intended to express the receding of awestruck admiration—stopped by the wall ! "

When informed that Mrs. Edgeworth was not her sister-authoress Miss Watts turned to Charlotte to give another demonstration. Corrected once more she looked round at Maria to see what sort of an animal she was and, " to make me some amends, she now drew her chair close to me and began to pour forth praises : ' Lady Delacour, O ! *Letters for Literary Ladies*, O ! ' "

Miss Watts might well say " O " for Lady Delacour. Jane Austen was, in all probability, also saying her "O" of admiration to the new circle of acquaintances she was making at Bath. For Lady Delacour, although not the heroine of *Belinda*, is certainly the character around whom most of the interest centres. Belinda herself is a pleasant young lady who does not deserve Maria's later disparagement. " I really was so provoked with the cold tameness of that stick or stone Belinda that I could have torn the pages to pieces." Belinda has been sent to stay with Lady Delacour in the hope that she will make a good match and, since Lady Delacour is the brilliant leader of London society, nothing seems more likely. The setting, that is to say, is the same as in a dozen other novels since *Evelina*. The great town house blazes with lights and laughter, the newspapers are full of Lady Delacour's parties, her dresses, her extravagances and her witticisms. But as soon as the party is over and the last carriage has rolled away and the servants go round putting out the lights, the animated face relaxes under its mask of paint and Lady Delacour walks up and down the empty, magnificent saloon, grappling her anguish in solitude. She has cancer of the breast. This, as for Proust, was Maria's symbol of the hidden corruption of society.

Lady Delacour's secret is shared by only one person, by Marriott her maid, who uses the knowledge as an instrument of tyranny. She removes the flowers, the jewels, the fancy costume while Lady Delacour sits with hollow cheeks and sunken eyes. She is resolved to endure any torture but the pity of the fashionable world which she despises. Yet it was the kind of life she understood, she felt fitted for no other and she feared the wholesale desertion of her friends which she felt would be the result if they learned of her disease. She refers to her husband Lord Delacour as " it " because he is carried in dead drunk in the early hours of every morning and does not seem to deserve the recognition of any human qualities that he may possess. A character out of Marmontel, he lives a life of brutish obstinacy because he has learned from his valet that the world thinks he is governed by his wife.

The most brilliant pages of the book are provided when Lady Delacour thinks fit to tell Belinda the story of her life. She is a remarkable creation coming from anyone's brain but she is all the more remarkable as coming from the brain of a writer who (save for the delinquency that *Castle Rackrent* represents) was concerned with the prosecution of education from the cradle to the grave. How Lady Delacour would have laughed ! Life is strange and irresistible, she seems to say, and there is no understanding or measuring the forces that govern human conduct. She is caught up by a destiny that is more powerful than herself ; she plays a role that she does not believe in and yet she fears to play any other. Dressed as a man she fights a duel with her greatest enemy Mrs. Luttridge, but even this swaggering boldness, we find, is largely bogus. Her clothes, her pistols and her courage have been supplied by her horsey, swearing, mannish friend, Mrs. Freke. (Mrs. Luttridge and Mrs. Freke seem to be something new in the novel—emancipated, harum-scarum women, semi-military, the female counterpart of the Regency buck.) " I am," said Lady Delacour to Belinda, " and I see you think me, a strange, weak, inconsistent creature. I was intended for something better, but now it is too late ; a coquette I have lived and a coquette I shall die."

Lady Delacour's stature as a character is due to very much more than the skull-beneath-the-flesh twist that is supplied by her attempt to conceal the disease that is killing her. Witty, ruthless, unkind, generous, repentant, she has qualities that make her commanding as a living woman ; that all this vivacity is set in the widest of all possible contexts gives her the dignity of a symbol. She is to die and the diversions and trivialities are diversions and trivialities no longer, they are a strong-minded woman's answer to the hate of the world, she is the *ancien régime* dying in glory and she is truly tragic.

The trouble is that she does not die.

The great talking-point about Maria Edgeworth's work has always been the extent to which her father interfered and whether or not his was a bad influence. On the one hand there are those who curse Edgeworth and say that never was there a clearer case of genuine creative talent being stifled by the censor. They can point to *Castle Rackrent*, in which Edgeworth had no hand whatsoever, and the irrepressible and highly individualistic tone of Maria's letters to show just what could be done when Maria was left to her own devices. On the other hand there is a growing body of opinion which, while admitting that her father's influence was sometimes unfortunate, claims that without her father's active encouragement Maria would never have been a writer at all.

" Whenever I thought of writing anything I always told him my first rough plans," Maria wrote in the *Memoirs*, " and always with the instinct of a good critic, he used to fix immediately upon that which would best answer the purpose. ' Sketch that and show it to me.' These words never failed to inspire me with hope of success. It was then sketched. Sometimes when I was too fond of a particular part, I used to dilate on it in the sketch ; but to this he always objected—' I don't want any of your painting—none of your drapery !—I can imagine all that !—let me see the bare skeleton.' Then he would in his own words fill up my sketch, paint the description or represent the character intended with such life that I was quite convinced he not only seized the ideas, but that he saw with the prophetic eye of taste the utmost that could be made of them. . . . I am sure that I could not have written or finished anything without his support."

All this is very interesting as showing us how Maria went to work. There is no doubt that Edgeworth had great gifts of invention which were used to extricate Maria from difficulties or absurdities ; what is more he had seen a great deal of the world and was able to supply her with grist for

the mill of her imagination. But Maria's testimony can
hardly be taken at its face value. In the first place it is not
true that she could not have written or finished anything
without his support. The conventional picture is of Maria
sitting in the library of Edgeworthstown and scratching
away with her pen while family life went on all around her.
Such a picture is substantially correct. But there were times
when she stole away to her own room to write stories and
plays of which her father had no knowledge until they were
finished. *Castle Rackrent* may have been written in this
way, *The Modern Griselda* certainly was. She arranged with
Johnson the publisher to have one copy printed without
her name on the title page, and this she presented to her
father in order to test his statement that he would know
her writing anywhere. It was a very tedious story about
female contrariness, but Edgeworth enjoyed it and, when
Maria told him her secret, was delighted that he had admired
the work without knowing its authoress. One of her
longest novels, *Helen*, was written fifteen years or so after
his death. No, given a certain amount of quiet encouragement of which most women writers in those days seemed to
stand in need (such is the distance we have travelled) Maria
would always have been a writer. She had learned to ride
a horse because her father had assumed that she would not
fall off, but more is needed for the writing for a novel than
Edgeworth's assumption that she could not fail.

Maria's deference to her father cannot be exaggerated. As
a child he ordered her, by way of a punishment for some
misdemeanour, to walk round a grass plot in the garden
until he came back from a visit that he was paying. He
had not anticipated being away long, but he was unexpectedly
delayed and Maria went on walking and walking, in implicit

obedience to his will, refusing even to pause and eat the luncheon that a servant brought from the house, until she was exhausted. It would have been surprising if Maria could have thought herself capable of lifting a finger without her father's intervention. But we should be taking too simple a view of the situation, and of the nature of creative imagination, if we were to believe her.

Belinda will always be a strong point in the case against Mr. Edgeworth, for there seems to be little doubt that he ruined it. The original sketch for *Belinda* was found among Maria's papers after her death and was quoted in full by her stepmother in the printed but unpublished *Life and Letters* of 1867. Maria's intention, we discover from this sketch, was for Lady Delacour to die. Following normal practice, however, the project was submitted to Mr. Edgeworth who immediately legislated that Lady Delacour was not to die, that the cancer of the breast was to be nothing but a nasty bruise which the learned Dr. X will cure for her, that the hard-bitten society woman should so far fall under the influence of the benign Belinda that she will repent of her ways, confide in her husband (who turns out to be an excellent fellow after all) and become, in the phrase of Marmontel, *la femme comme il y en a peu*. So much on the authority of Mrs. Barbauld who was a very good friend of the Edgeworths and included *Belinda* in her celebrated fifty-volume series of the British novelists. It was Mr. Edgeworth also, it appears, who suddenly thought fit to transform Clarence Hervey, hitherto an agreeable but not very sensible man-about-town, into the preposterous Mr. Thomas Day, complete with wife-training establishment; though true enough, as some concession to what may the more easily be believed, there is only one trainee instead of

two. Virginia (she has this appropriate name) turns out to
be in love with the picture of a handsome sailor and Hervey
is then free to marry the modest Belinda. Maria's fine
conception has been deflated.

But it is still a brilliant novel. Together with *Cecilia* and
Camilla Jane Austen referred to it as a " work in which the
greatest powers of the mind are displayed, the most thorough
knowledge of human nature, the happiest delineation of its
varieties, the liveliest effusions of wit and humour, are
conveyed to the world in the best chosen language." After
Lady Delacour herself one can well imagine that Jane Austen
took the greatest delight in Sir Philip Baddeley, a fop and a
fool, the sort of creature upon whom women writers had
been getting their revenge for the past thirty years. He is a
joyful creation in self-satisfied idiocy, and his proposal of
marriage to Belinda Portman is something to set beside
Mr. Collins' proposal in *Pride and Prejudice*. His animated
description of the fêtes at Frogmore is worth quoting.

> " O damme ! but I would have driven you in my curricle,"
> said Sir Philip, " it was the finest sight and best conducted I
> ever saw, and only wanted Miss Portman to make it complete.
> We had gipsies, and Mrs. Mills the actress for the queen of the
> gipsies ; and she gave us a famous good song, *Rochfort,* you
> know—and then there *was* two children upon an *ass*—damme,
> I don't know how they came there, for they're things one sees
> every day—and belonged only to two of the soldiers' wives—
> for we had the whole band of the Staffordshire playing at
> dinner, and we had some famous glees—and Fawcett gave us
> his laughing song, and then we had the launching of the ship,
> and only it was a boat, it would have been well enough—but
> damme, the song of *Polly Oliver* was worth the whole, except
> the Flemish Hercules, Ducrow, you know, dressed in light blue
> and silver, and—Miss Portman, I wish you had seen this—three
> great coach wheels on his chin, and a ladder and two chairs

and two children on them—and after that, he sported a musquet and bayonet, with the point of the bayonet on his chin—faith ! that was really famous ! But I forgot the Pyrrhic dance, Miss Portman, which was damned fine too—danced in boots and spurs by those Hungarian fellows—they jump and turn about, and clap their knees with their hands, and put themselves in all sorts of ways—and then we had that song of *Polly Oliver,* as I told you before, and Mrs. Mills gave us—no, no—it was a drummer of the Staffordshire dressed as a gipsy girl, gave us *The cottage on the moor,* the most charming thing, and would suit your voice, Miss Portman—damme, you'd sing it like an angel.—But where was I ? O, then they had tea—and fireplaces built of brick, out in the air—and then the entrance to the ballroom was all a colonnade done with lamps and flowers, and that sort of thing—and there was some bon-mot (but that was in the morning) amongst the gipsies about an orange, and the stadtholder—and then there was a Turkish dance, all very fine, but nothing to come up to the Pyrrhic touch, which was a great deal the most knowing, in boots and spurs—damme, now I can't describe the thing to you, 'tis a cursed pity you weren't there, damme."

Lady Delacour is a character in conflict with herself, inhibited by her fear of ridicule, at the same time envious and contemptuous of ordinary morality. And whereas all this is easy enough for the novelist to express when Lady Delacour is in the mood of the confessional, when she is telling Belinda the story of her life, it is quite another matter to express Lady Delacour's inner contentions in the more dramatic give and take of conversation where she is quite obviously saying one thing and meaning another. Maria never did anything better in this way than the scene between Lady Delacour and her daughter Helen, a child whom she has neglected in order to pursue her life of fashion. Belinda, with the help of Clarence Hervey, contrives to bring the child unexpectedly into her presence. But Lady Delacour treats her daughter with coldness. She corrects her grammar and tells her it is ill-bred to begin sentences and not finish them. What is more there is no need for Helen to observe a ceremony towards her mother she does not feel. And she cross-examines Helen until the child is on the point of tears. In a burst of generous feeling Lady Delacour says that she is one of the sweetest girls in the world, and Helen springs forward to kiss her mother. She presses close to her mother's bosom, clasping her with all her force ; then Lady Delacour screams and pushes her daughter away.

The Edgeworths arrived in Paris in the late October of 1802. The warmth with which they were received would have surprised anyone but Mr. Edgeworth, who had reserves of calm with which to face even the most excessive marks of favour. They were admitted to the most exclusive literary and scientific circles, Edgeworth was made a member of the *Societé d'Encouragement pour l'Industrie*, Maria received homage as an educationist and as a novelist. What is most noticeable to us, at a distance of a century and a half, is the sense of a genuine European culture which arises from everything that we can learn about this extraordinary period of remission between two long stretches of warfare. In the days before total war, it seems, it only needed the signing of a peace for French and British society to intermingle without any embarrassment. Everyone subscribed to the belief that civilisation (and there was general agreement about the meaning of the term) embraced them all. It transcended the nation. Perhaps it was for the last time. James Watt was there to advise on some engineering works, a Dr. Maclean arrived to gather statistics on French suicides, Herschel was there and they (with Edgeworth among them) were meeting, on the most agreeable terms, such prominent French scientists as Berthollet, Montgolfier and Breguet. When Napoleon suddenly took it into his head that Edgeworth was brother to the celebrated Abbé Edgeworth(who had received Louis XVI's last confession) and ordered him to leave Paris within twenty-four hours, a number of eminent Frenchmen signed a petition on his behalf and Edgeworth was allowed to return. Revolutions and wars might come, but civilisation went on and the fireworks began every night at half past ten.

From Madame d'Ouditot Maria heard anecdotes of Rousseau. The beautiful Madame Récamier who was herself one of the sights of Paris took the Edgeworths to the dingy rooms where La Harpe lived and persuaded him to recite his verses for them, they met Madame de Genlis (Maria took an instant dislike to the great pedagogue), struck up a friendship with Madame Delessert who had been the benefactress of Rousseau, Monsieur and Madame Suard, Madame de Pastoret (she was the first to establish infant schools in France) and the celebrated Abbé Morellet (of whom Maria wrote to her aunt—" O ! my dear Aunt Mary, how you would love that man, and we need not be afraid of loving him, for he is near eighty ! ") The Louvre was filled with the spoils of Napoleon's campaigns and Maria almost broke her neck looking at the pictures. She caught a glimpse of a little man with a pale face riding a white horse at a military review ; even Mr. Edgeworth himself saw no more of Napoleon for he had come to the opinion that the man was an enemy to liberty and, although arrangements had been made, declined the honour of being presented.

In the middle of all this excitement it was appropriate that Maria should receive an offer of marriage. She was

thirty-five, had never received an offer before and was
never to receive one again. He was a certain M. Edelcrantz,
a Swedish gentleman " of superior understanding and mild
manners " then in the service of the King of Sweden. The
fourth Mrs. Edgeworth has put it on record as her opinion
that Maria was exceedingly in love with M. Edelcrantz and,
by way of proof, mentions an incident that took place shortly
afterwards. Maria, Charlotte and she were in a shop making
some purchases but Maria sat apart, lost in thought. " Her
father came in and stood opposite to her but she did not
see him until he spoke to her, when she started and burst
into tears." Ever afterwards, the unexpected mention of
Sweden was enough to put her into confusion though Maria
declared very firmly that she never felt for him anything
but esteem and gratitude ; in any case, nothing would
tempt her to leave her own dear friends and her own country
to live in Sweden.

It would be wrong to make too much of the incident.
Back home in Ireland, it is true, Maria certainly preserved
enough warmth for M. Edelcrantz to write a novel, *Leonora*,
with a view to be pleasing what she imagined to be his
tastes. These must have been very old-fashioned tastes for
it is the story of the manner in which a faithful, prudent
and almost inhumanly chilling wife wins back her faithless,
erring husband ; the means are those of uncomplaining
moral superiority. This, surely, was the least that Maria
could do for the only man who had confessed his love
for her. He never married and Maria never knew
whether he ever saw the work she had written to please
him. He was, it seems, a surprisingly ugly man and
Edgeworth teased her unmercifully on what he called her
" preferences."

Tales of Fashionable Life were issued in six volumes, the first three in 1809 and the second three in 1812. It is their misfortune and a critic's convenience that they can, all too easily, be pigeon-holed under a number of neat labels : Learn how to say No ! (*Vivian*), Be Alert to Avoid Boredom (*Ennui*), Be Prompt to Pay your Debts (*The Dun*), Be Above Intriguing for Advantage (*Manœuvering*), Shun Empty Ambition (*Almeria*), and so on. Yet they were extraordinarily popular with her contemporaries and, though this was not a factor that weighed with Maria, for the first time she began to draw really big royalties.

They are fairy tales that refuse to confess. They do not have the good manners to begin with " Once upon a time " or " Let's pretend." The real-seeming world they pretend to describe is all the more illusory for not having an ogre and a sugar-plum common. Every child (and some fortunate grown-ups) know how real the ogres and the dragons can be —they are real as the imagination itself is real, " everything possible to be believed is an image of the truth "—but a drearily utilitarian story in which the pure in heart prosper and the wicked meet with disaster seems not only to be untrue to the world as we know it but to insult, by its very single-mindedness, our own efforts to lead happy, healthy and wealthy lives.

The moral earnestness that lay behind the *Tales of Fashionable Life* would have crippled a lesser writer. But Maria's natural exuberance repeatedly came to rescue her from the most unpromising situations and though her characters are rarely anything but puppets they wear their paint a little more brightly than those of, say, Mrs. Chapone, their jig is a little gayer, and they squeak out their parts with greater conviction even though what they have to say is only " I really must know my own mind," or " Boredom is bad for me."

But life, we protest, is very much more mysterious than this. It is splashed with blood, lit with fire, it is dark, it is bright, even within the limits of polite society during the early years of the nineteenth century men must have been puzzled by the inconsistencies of what they took to be the working of a moral order. There were conflicts and mysteries even under a satin waistcoat. The least we can ask of our serious writer, then (we exclude the comic writer, that most intellectual of beings, because we forgive anyone who amuses us), is that he should be occasionally puzzled.

Not at all, Maria seems to say. Listen !

When Richard Lovell Edgeworth's mother lay dying she summoned her son to her bedside and said, " My son, learn early how to say no." She very much mistook her son's character, for if ever there was a man who knew his own mind it was he : he knew it to the exclusion of the minds of others. So much so that he allowed himself the luxury of passing on what was substantially the same advice to Maria when his own turn came to die. Of Maria he thought she was weak and generous when, as subsequent events showed, she was as strong-willed as her father. The ability to say no was an Edgeworth characteristic, and when Maria was looking round for a theme for a novel nothing was more natural than it should be resorted to. Know your own mind. Life is no more mysterious than that. And it was in this way that the idea for *Vivian* came to her.

Taken together, *Vivian* and *Ennui* show most of the weaknesses and most of the strengths of the *Fashionable Tales*—tales, it must never be forgotten, that were written to warn people against the faults they displayed. As so often happens,

the " period " of the novels is that of Mr. Edgeworth's
prime (this is still more noticeable in *Ormond*, which treats
of a time when he was in his twenties) when, as no doubt
he told his daughter, it was the " fashion of the times for the
gentlemen to pay exclusive attention to the matrons. Few
of the young men seemed to think it worth while to speak
to an unmarried woman in any company " : and an election
of the year '40 could be remembered without any great
straining by one of the characters.

Vivian is the heir to a large fortune, has a doting mother
anxious for him to marry wealth and rank, and a friend
and one-time tutor, Russell, who is anxious only that Vivian
should be *prudent* ; he has keen understanding of the
instability of Vivian's character. The objection to the
story, and to many another of Maria's tales, is that the hero's
leading characteristic (in this case weakness of will) is so
much the most important part of the narrative that the
incidents are contrived, and contrived for this purpose alone,
to show the defect in action. He is so busy being irresolute
that there is no time for him to be a human being, although
(and this was because Maria was a very gifted writer) he
always threatens to be. At enormous cost he begins to
transform his charming modern house into a Gothic castle ;
the idea had been his originally, but the prudent Russell had
pointed out the absurdity of the enterprise and he would
have consented to give it up had not Russell gone away
and other advisers taken his place. " It was not, therefore,
to please his own taste that he ran into this imprudent
expense, but merely to gratify the taste of others." The
next step in his downfall is when he allows himself to be
persuaded to stand for Parliament where he meets a political
opportunist called Wharton. Poor Vivian is now seduced

by Wharton's wife (once again he cannot say No). Nevertheless he has retained his political integrity. He speaks and votes after his own conscience, follows no party, and wins a reputation for himself as a patriot. This, however, is merely an eminence to which he has been raised by Maria for the pleasure of hurling him down. He marries Lady Sarah Lydhurst (she is passionately in love with him and, although he doesn't like her, he cannot say No) and finds himself embroiled by his father-in-law, Lord Glistonbury, in a political intrigue from which only resolution could extricate him. He weakly gives way, challenges Wharton to a duel, is shot and killed and, if that is not enough punishment for his irresolution, his wife gave birth to a dead son and " has never since appeared in what is called the WORLD." (If a pregnant woman went through any mental distress in the year 1809 her child was always born dead.)

If we were contemporaries of Maria Edgeworth and had the hardihood to challenge the theme of *Vivian* it would have been by no means impossible to find her replying : " It is no more than the theme of *Hamlet*. I am not vain enough to think that my work can be spoken of in the same breath as Shakespeare's. But if you approve the theme of *Hamlet* how can you disapprove the theme of *Vivian* ? "

To our way of thinking this only reveals the superficiality of Maria, but the different impulses that lie behind *Hamlet* and *Vivian* would not have been so apparent to many intelligent minds of the late eighteenth century—and Maria was a very intelligent woman indeed. There was nothing tentative or exploratory about her work ; it was a statement. The instrument of man's perfectibility lay within his own power, and if he was a rogue he was all the greater rogue for having had the choice of good and evil and neglected to choose wisely. It was the very fault for which Rosamond had been punished when she chose the purple jar. Maria would have found it hard to believe that Shakespeare did not share this view of human nature.

Against this must be set the fact that the very exigencies of the moral story led Maria into fields where, had she looked upon the novel with the same eyes as Jane Austen, she would never have ventured. Quite apart from the political and professional scenes of such later works as *Patronage* she found herself led to the creation of new characters within the framework of the old novel of manners, new, living women who (almost to Maria's surprise, we feel) thrust themselves into the world by reason of the demands of her very rigidity ; rather as a poet will find himself writing a poem that changes under the exigencies of rhyme and prosody.

Such a character is Lady Sarah, Vivian's wife. At the beginning of the story she is a cold stick of a creature who, when her admirer dies of a chill " was precisely as sorry as decorum required." The plot requires it of her. Maria's ingenuity (or Mr. Edgeworth's) must have been considerably exercised by the problem of so manipulating matters for Vivian to contract a disastrous marriage (simply because he cannot say No) since one of the necessary preliminaries, according to convention, was a certain degree of propinquity over a period of time when he pays attentions to Lady Sarah which she regards as homage and he does not regard as insincere. Obviously this can only be done if she is cold and unresponsive. " Lady Sarah Lidhurst," he remarks, " has no thoughts or feelings, no more than an automaton. I'll answer for her—I'm sure I can do her the justice to proclaim, that she has always, from the very first moment I saw her till this instant, conducted herself towards me with the same petrified and petrifying propriety."

The marriage (brought about by her father's manipulation and her own nervous breakdown) is necessary to the plot ; but what is not at all necessary and what immediately becomes manifest is Maria's understanding of a fiercely inhibited nature like Lady Sarah's which has suddenly achieved the object of its desire. There is something almost frightening in her passion. Vivian was overwhelmed. For her " duty and passion now had the same object." She is fiercely jealous, she is monopolistic, she can hardly bear that he should leave the house without her ; and then she reproaches him with, " Ah, you would have been much happier if you hadn't married me." Yet when Vivian makes his final mistake and sells his political integrity to save himself from bankruptcy and help her father to a new title, she falls on her knees and begs him to sell everything they have, plate, furniture, equipage, house, sell everything rather than his honour.

It is a surprising outburst, but then Lady Sarah has developed into a surprising figure. Had Maria been merely a didactic writer Lady Sarah would have remained narrow-minded, a scold, perhaps a spendthrift. As it is she is a figure with true possibilities of tragedy (the modern novelist would have built his book around her), she is the only character in the book who really catches at our sympathy, and she is real when the moral necessity for her to be otherwise had spent itself. She is the creation of a didactic exigency, the flower growing out of the up-ended drainpipe in the garden.

Satire was a word that Maria abhorred. To her ear it implied malice and exaggeration. To say that her satirical portraits are among her best would have shocked her immeasurably. But what else are we to say about such a creature as Lord Glistonbury ? In the twentieth century politics might have proved a little too exacting for him (or would they ?). But we really see him as some big figure on the Black Market. He is proud of his shadiness, proud of his wild oats, yet he pays suitable deference to progressive ideas in education. He lectures the prospective tutor of his son Lidhurst. " Now, my idea for Lidhurst is simply this : that he should know everything that is in all the best books in the library, but yet that he should be the farthest possible from a book-worm—that he should never, except in a set speech in the House, have the air of having opened a book in his life—mother wit for me !—in most cases—and that easy style of originality, which shows the true gentleman. As to morals—Lidhurst, walk on, my boy—as to morals, I confess I couldn't bear to see anything of the Joseph Surface about him."

The foibles of society provided her with a great deal of the best of her material and, if she was ever in doubt, she could transfer the scene to the other side of St. George's Channel, to territory where she reigned supreme. When she proposed the social malady of ennui to herself for the medicine of fiction she feared that the remedy might prove worse than the disease ; a prize essay on the same subject had once put the adjudicating committee of the Academy of Berlin to sleep. But once in Ireland Maria knew that she could bore nobody.

The story is told in the first person by the Earl of Glenthorn. After 12,000 words or so in England, during which Glenthorn contracts an unfortunate marriage and Maria shows an unusual knowledge of the diversions

5

and dissipations to which a young man of title and wealth might betake him in order to relieve his oppressive boredom (prize fighting on breezy commons, gambling in rooms by the light of candles, the shutters being drawn so that the gamblers would remain unaware of the passing of the nights and days) Glenthorn transports himself to his Irish estates. The journey through the Irish countryside where he is driven by mad coachmen in broken-down coaches to noisome inns where no food but a bottle of whisky could be obtained was quite sufficient in itself to cause some lifting of the fog of apathy. *Ennui* is a very readable novel because the very nature of the cure (work, diversion, danger and eventually the loss of Glenthorn's title and estates) could so easily have gone to make a story with a less serious purpose. Glenthorn makes plenty of mistakes, of course ; he builds fine new cottages for people who do not appreciate them, he has the wrong ideas about encouraging local industry, and so on. M'Leod, his Scotch agent, has every one of the Edgeworth ideas about estate management and because they were very sensible ideas M'Leod is a very sensible (and very likable, very Scotch) character, too.

The real cause of ennui, however, was title and estates so long as the holder regards them as an excuse for doing nothing useful with his time. So just when we are beginning to entertain the greatest hopes of Glenthorn's recovery (he has been enlivened by the attempts of rebels upon his life) it turns out that he is not the rightful earl at all. The old nurse had changed the babies in the cradle and the rightful earl is honest Christy, the local blacksmith. Glenthorn, or Donoghoe as we are now to call him, is thrown upon his own resources, applies himself to the study of law for a number of years, achieves success, marries the heir-at-law to the Glenthorn estates and, when the rightful Earl expresses a wish to go back to the blacksmith's shop, returns to the castle with the firm intention of being as much like Mr. Edgeworth as possible. The imagination is defeated by the thought of what would have happened had Maria decided that ennui was too powerful for the means to cure it. We are grateful for the happy ending.

It is no coincidence, therefore, that the best of these *Tales of Fashionable Life* should be *The Absentee*. If stories with a purpose have to be written this is the way to write them. It has all the advantages of *Ennui* in that a great deal of the setting is in Ireland, and it has also the advantages of *Vivian* in that the demands of her moral led her to the creation of a set of forceful characters. But it is moralising with a difference. It is doubtful whether Maria realised the difference between a moral tale that sprang from some abstract idea and one that sprang from an observable situation ; and we should possibly be wrong to press the difference for there is no strict dividing line. But whereas *The Absentee* arose from a great contemporary abuse—the Irish landowners living in London while their agents mulcted the peasantry of money that would eventually be thrown away on the gambling table—*Ennui, Vivian* and so many others sprang from a Puritan system of moral precepts, and it is hard to resist the idea that this has a great deal to do with their respective merits.

The Absentee was originally written as a play but when Edgeworth tried to get it produced in London Sheridan made the excuse that the Lord Chamberlain would never license it. Maria therefore began to incorporate the idea into her long and ambitious novel *Patronage* at which she had been labouring for some time. But when the publisher

began clamouring for another tale to fill up a volume she
excised it from the bulk of *Patronage* and worked it up into
the form in which we now have it. She wrote with her
mouth full of some strong lotion to allay the pangs of toothache. Though toothache was very much more unpleasant
for Maria than moral earnestness the result is very much
more agreeable to the reader. *The Absentee* is, together with
Castle Rackrent, generally reckoned to be Maria's best work.

Its great triumph is Lady Clonbrony who insists on living
in the fashionable world of London even though her husband
has a sneaking desire to return to Ireland and "retrench" and
although they are living far above their incomes. She is an
Irishwoman who is ashamed to be thought provincial and
goes through agonies to look, speak, move and breathe like
an Englishwoman. " You *cawnt* conceive the *peens* she *teekes*
to talk of the *teebles* and *cheers* and to thank Q, and with so
much *teeste*, to speak pure English," remarks one of her
enemies. But the very malice of such women only makes
us sympathise with Lady Clonbrony who, in spite of her
vulgarity and her ability to swallow any insult provided it
will further her social ambitions, is a warmly human character.

She gave a splendid gala with the object of impressing
the fashionable world.

> One young lady expressed her astonishment so audibly as
> to attract the notice of all the bystanders. Lady Clonbrony,
> delighted, seized both her hands, shook them and laughed
> heartily ; then, as the young lady with her party passed on,
> her ladyship recovered herself, drew up her head and said to
> the company near her, " Poor thing ! I hope I covered her
> little naiveté properly. How new she must be."

Brilliant as the London scenes are it is when Lady Clonbrony's son, Lord Colambre, arrives in Ireland to make an

inspection of of his own and his father's estates incognito that Maria's inventive fun is seen at its best. Summer lightning plays over the gimcrack Irish country mansions, places that had been commenced as though their owners had the resources of the mines of Peru and finished as though they hadn't sixpence ; a country where improvidence is the poetry of the financially embarrassed, where a man, faced by the visit of an English lord, will sit down with a pencil and paper to calculate which would cost him least : to put his house in fit state to receive his visitor, or to burn it to the ground—and deciding in favour of the burning. Dublin is full of the new rich who go in for the most modern and most sensational vulgarity. Mrs. Rafferty, the wife of a Dublin grocer, has a country villa called Tusculum which possesses " a little conservatory, and a little pinery, and a little grapery, and a little aviary, and a little pheasantry, and a little dairy for show, and a little cottage for ditto, with a grotto full of shells, and a little hermitage full of earwigs, and a little ruin full of looking glass, ' to enlarge and multiply the effects of the Gothic.' "

In case we should suspect that Maria believes that oddity is confined to the new rich we are taken to Halloran Castle where the Count, in a gold-laced hat and long skirts to his laced waistcoat lived in company with an eagle, a goat, a dog, an otter, several gold and silver fish in a glass globe, a white mouse in a cage and the great skeletons of an elk and a moose-deer. These last Lord Colambre surveyed " with that sense of awe and admiration by which a superior mind is always struck on beholding any of the great works of providence."

It was still a time, of course, when a character in a novel was designed to appeal to the emotions of the reader, to his (or more frequently her) admiration, envy, hate, contempt, or to the reader's sense of superiority or of the ridiculous ; and, of all these, the most difficult to create was the hero or heroine, an undertaking in which even Sir Walter Scott so frequently fell down. In *The Absentee* Maria presents us with one of her most attractive heroines ; she is intelligent, witty, not spectacularly beautiful and with as little priggishness (the curse of such characters) as Elizabeth Bennet herself. But Grace Nugent is, after all, nobody. She is the ward of Lady Clonbrony but she has no fortune and there is some obscurity about her birth. Many a great lady who can be condescending and familiar to her in private is aloof and afraid of committing herself even with a nod of recognition when in company. On such occasions Grace could be crushing. She would wait until the room was quite silent and then lean forward to the great lady, screening her whisper with her hand. " Lady Langdale, you may curtsey to me now. Nobody is looking."

Lord Colambre is not, unfortunately, free from a certain stiffness which his detractors would call priggishness. Although not yet twenty-one he followed the charitable rule of believing only one half of what the world said. He has such a keen eye for insincerity that, at such times, we suspect that a sort of Edgeworth mist is floating across the page, that Maria is writing what is desirable rather than what is true. But it is only a mist. In a moment it has passed and we find him falling half in love with the beautiful Lady Isabel even though he knows that she is a thoroughly bad character and that her mother is angling for the match.

The one discordant note in the novel is Colambre's conduct when he discovers that Grace Nugent, with whom he has now fallen in love, is illegitimate. " Lord Colambre had the greatest dread of marrying any woman whose mother had conducted herself ill. His reason, his prejudices, his pride, his delicacy and even his limited experience were all against it. All his hopes, his plans for future happiness, were shaken to their very foundation ; he felt that he had received a blow that stunned his mind, and from which he could not recover his faculties."

That this was quite unreasonable never seems to have occured to Maria or the censor, her father. To them, even though Grace had not been brought up by her mother, had been subject to no evil influence, this revelation of her origin precipitates a Great Crisis. For a family with such a passionate belief in education this was very inconsistent. It seems probable that the inconsistency was pointed out to Maria, for when *Patronage* was published in the following year she went out of her way to rectify what was admittedly an error. *Patronage* had, however, been on the stocks for a number of years and it might be possible to show that the passage about illegitimacy was written before *The Absentee*. But whatever the truth of the matter Colambre's prejudice robs him of our sympathy just at a time when he is most in need of it.

Matters are not helped at all by the fact that Grace Nugent, restored to legitimacy and a great fortune for the purpose of a happy ending, should acknowledge his right to such an opinion. Maria treated her heroine very shabbily indeed, almost as shabbily as the Jewess in *Harrington* (a novel written to show that Jews were quite as nice as the rest of us) who is turned into a Christian in the last few pages of the book so that the hero can marry her without losing caste. *Harrington* is not a novel to take very seriously, but *The Absentee* is, and one can only deplore the opportunity that Maria missed not only of showing how a spirited young lady could stand

up to a really intimidating situation but also (and this may
have seemed of more importance to Mr. Edgeworth) of
setting down some of the Edgeworthian principles of
education. No doubt such conduct was not expected of a
heroine of fiction. Her acquiescence in Colambre's stupidity
is a sad falling off from the vigorous, lively creature she is
revealed to us in the first part. If she had remained illegitimate, and, by force of her personality, made Colambre
confess that he was wrong, it would have humanised his
rather complacent lordship. But Mr. Edgeworth would not
have permitted this.

It was Ruskin's opinion that more could be learned of
Irish politics by reading *The Absentee* than from a thousand
columns of Blue books. Lord Macaulay was another en-
thusiast. The scene where Lord Colambre reveals his identity
to the rascally agent was the best thing, he said, since Homer
wrote the XXII book of the *Odyssey*. But it is less for any
political consideration, or even for the scene where Clonbrony unmasks himself, that we read *The Absentee* to-day.
It is for the wonderful sureness of the portrait of Lady
Clonbrony, of her husband's friend, Sir Terence O'Fay
("likewise written off, not philosophically constructed,"
said Maria, "whilst I was writing him I always saw him
and heard him speak.") for Larry the coachman, and for
Mrs. Rafferty's dinner party of profusion and pretension
where she shrieks at the blunders of her untrained servants
and calls out to her husband, "Corny Rafferty, Corny
Rafferty, you're no more *gud* at the *fut* of my table than a
stick of celery !"

It was a good idea (and Mr. Edgeworth's at that, too !) to
conclude the book with a letter from Larry the coachman
to his brother in London. Only Larry's simple mind would

think that the return of the Clonbronys to Ireland meant the inauguration of a new heaven and a new earth, and little short of this as a conclusion for a novel would satisfy the contemporary reader. *The Absentee* is a fine novel. Had the other *Tales of Fashionable Life* been up to this standard Mme. de Stael would have spared us her celebrated reproach, " *Vraiment, Miss Edgeworth est digne de l'enthousiasme mais elle se perd dans votre triste utilité.*"

Maria was to complete two more novels of first importance before the death of her father in 1817, and in both of them he had a considerable hand. Of *Patronage*, it is true, he wrote not a word ; but the idea, the general scheme was his. As long ago as 1787 he had amused Mrs. Elizabeth Edgeworth, then recovering from childbirth, with the story of the Freeman family which he made up as he went along. This story, which Maria set down on paper, was of two families, one making their way in the world by their own effort and the other depending upon the favour of the great. On this foundation Maria built her long novel.

In Maria's opinion her father's story was very much better than hers : " His hero and heroine were in greater difficulties than mine, more in love and consequently more interesting, and the whole story was infinitely more entertaining." The novel gave Maria very much more difficulty than anything else she ever wrote, as well it might for the subject was one of extraordinary difficulty, involving as it did following up the professional careers of the members of two families. It meant incursions into the church, the army, law and medicine ; it was a project that might have daunted a bolder writer. Whatever one feels constrained to say about Edgeworth's influence on his daughter's writing the probability is that *Patronage* is the kind of novel that would have been quite impossible for her without his active help.

"He left me always at full liberty to use or reject his hints," Maria wrote, "throwing new materials before me continually with the profusion of genius and of affection. There was no danger of offending or disappointing him by not using what he offered. . . . He forgot his gifts almost as soon as he had made them—thought the ideas were mine, if they appeared before him in any form in which he liked them ; and if never used, he never missed, never thought of inquiring for them. Continually he supplied new observations on every passing occurrence, and wakened the attention with anecdotes of the living or of the dead."

But while it is easy enough to pass on anecdotes (of which Edgeworth had an extraordinary store) it is a very different matter to pass on the particular quality of experience which a writer requires to make use of those anecdotes and build them into the full structure of a novel. It is surprising, therefore, that the one character in *Patronage* which Maria said was entirely her own invention, is one for whose creation is demanded that very sense of experience which Maria could hardly be expected to have by nature and which her father could hardly communicate by anecdote. This is Lord Oldborough, Minister of the Crown, and an imposing figure out of eighteenth-century politics. He is solid, three-dimensional, a master of political intrigue, a man who suffers from no delusions and is therefore never surprised by treachery ; he is unscrupulous and quick to anger, supremely self-confident, of great personal bravery, contemptuous of the mob and a hater of democracy. Yet he has great nobility of mind and is unswervingly faithful to his sovereign.

There is a characteristic scene when a hostile mob gathered

round his carriage as he was returning home late one day. His conduct is just what we would expect from our previous view of the man as he dealt with the less sensational day-to-day affairs of the first minister of the crown. The incident is confirmatory, not revelatory.

Lord Oldborough now listened to their execrations, till from abuse they began to proceed to outrage. Stones were thrown at his carriage. One of his servants narrowly escaped being struck. Lord Oldborough was alone—he threw open his carriage door, and sprang out on the step.

" Whose life is it you seek ? " cried he, in a voice which obtained instant silence. " Lord Oldborough's ? Lord Oldborough stands before you. Take his life who dares—a life spent in your service. Strike ! But strike openly. You are Englishmen, not assassins."

Then, turning to his servants, he added, in a calm voice, " Home—slowly. Not a man here will touch you. Keep your master in sight. If I fall, mark by what hand."

Then, stepping down into the midst of the people, he crossed the street to the flagged pathway, the crowd opening to make way for him. He walked on with a deliberate, firm step ; the mob moving along with him, sometimes huzzaing, sometimes uttering horrid execrations in horrid tones. Lord Oldborough, preserving absolute silence, still walked on, never turned his head, or quickened his pace, till he reached his own house. Then, facing the mob, as he stood waiting till the door should be opened, the people, struck with his intrepidity, with one accord joined in a shout of applause.

The next instant and before the door was opened, they cried, " Hat off !—Hat off ! "

Lord Oldborough's hat never stirred. A man took up a stone. " Mark that man ! " cried Lord Oldborough.

The door opened. " Return to your homes my countrymen, and bless God that you have not any of you to answer this night for murder ! "

Then entering his house, he took off his hat, and gave it to one of his attendants.

Although it is quite possible that this incident came straight out of Maria's imagination (indeed, she stated quite categorically that her father had no hand in the writing of the book) it has the true ring of an anecdote by Richard Lovell Edgeworth. There are plenty of examples in the *Memoirs* for comparison. Or, if not from her father, the incident may have been based upon some happening in one of those interminable volumes of memoirs and reminiscences of which Maria was such an omnivorous reader. There is a note of veracity about the event that deepens from sentence to sentence (even more powerful in the proper context) until the hostility of the mob changes to applause. The sudden cry for Oldborough to remove his hat (the mob turns playful, they want to humiliate him) is the authentic touch of the eye-witness account. It pulls one up with a jerk. We would like more made of it. We should like to be sure that Maria understood all the implications of what she was writing. Normally, as she regretfully wrote to Mrs. Barbauld, she left little to the imagination. Her novels were filled with heavily underlined incidents so that when, as here, one is allowed to speak for itself the effect is arresting.

The scene comes more than three-quarters of the way through the book and it is some measure of the success of Maria's presentation of Oldborough that it is inconceivable that he should act in any other way. If the incident is entirely invented she has to be given full credit for a nervous accuracy and an economy she too rarely permitted herself ; and, if borrowed, we must recognise the skill with which a patch of reality has been incorporated into the very stuff of the novel, tearing none away. The stature of a novelist is not to be gauged by his ability to invent anecdote—some of the best have been the least inventive—but it may often

be judged by the use he makes of it. When Lord Oldborough's hat refused to stir it sent a vibration, out of
the depths of the writer's experience, through the whole
novel.

The general idea of *Patronage*—Edgeworth's idea—is
unfair. Two teams of human beings, two families, set off
in the race towards success, the Percys and the Falconers.
At the weigh-in everything seems fair enough ; the teams
are as equal as though Maria had picked them herself :
father and mother, three sons and two daughters on each
side. The Percys, however, scorn patronage. They rely on
their own abilities, and since they are a very clever family
this is very wise of them. The Falconers, on the other hand,
rely entirely on patronage, and since they are not at all clever
this is very wise of them. That the Percys win through to
success and the Falconers, after great initial success, are ruined
proves nothing about patronage. If the Percys had allowed
Oldborough to help them as much as he helped the Falconers
their rise to fame and fortune would have come about all
the quicker ; and had the Falconers refused that help they
would never have risen at all. There is no more to it than
that.

Maria must often have reflected that bad characters are
frequently so much more interesting than good characters.
Buckhurst Falconer, lazy, irresolute, dissipated, warm-
hearted, is a much more solid and convincing human being
than his more successful rivals, the three brothers Percy ;
and Mrs. Falconer with her two silly daughters provide
much better reading than do Mrs. Percy and her two
daughters who are, we discover, none other than our old
acquaintances the wise parent and the two contrasting
daughters of Maria's tales for children. Rosamond has

even been allowed to keep her old name, but Laura has
been rechristened Caroline. She is, however, still the same
very prudent, self-contained, perfectly poised young lady as
ever. Rosamond, who very endearingly confessed that she
wanted to marry a hero and be a heroine herself, probably
said the truth about her sister Caroline when, in the most
loving and gently chiding manner imaginable, she said :
" Bless me, Caroline, if you are so prudent at eighteen what
will you be at thirty ? Beware !—and in the meantime
remember that you will never be a heroine—what a stupid,
uninteresting heroine you will make ! You will never get
into any entanglements, never have any adventures. . . .
Recollect that Dr. Johnson, when his learned sock was off,
confessed that he could never be thoroughly interested in
Clarissa because he knew that her prudence would always
be equal to every occasion."

Knowing the worst about her own heroine Maria per-
sisted. What is more, she gave her the perfect Edgeworth
hero, a certain Count Altenberg, but nothing is less endearing
about Maria's good characters than their calculation. Before
falling in love with anyone they bring out a moral tape-
measure and give the prospective husband or wife a complete
check-up to see whether they come up to specification.
Then, and only then, is emotion unleashed.

Discovering that a certain beautiful lady is the daughter of
a divorced woman and, what is more, has been brought up
by her (an improvement this on *The Absentee*), one of the
young Percys instantly drops all interest. He does not even
bother to enquire whether the father or mother had been
the guilty party. He closes his mind. But Count Altenberg
is even more calculating than young Percy. He is determined
to discover whether or not the beautiful Caroline is capable

of mean passion—of jealousy, for example. By applauding the acting of a young lady whom Caroline might have some cause for regarding as her rival in the Count's affections, he puts Caroline to what he considers a very severe test. How can she support, for one moment, the applause that the handsome and wealthy count is giving to her rival? But Caroline comes through the test with flying colours, and before the last act of the play comes round the Count cannot forgive himself for ever having supposed that Caroline could be liable to any of the foibles of her sex. It does not improve matters, from our point of view, to think that Caroline herself would have approved such a test.

A fortnight before Mr. Edgeworth died on June 13, 1817 Maria was able to place in his hands the first hundred and sixty printed pages of *Ormond* which the publisher had good-naturedly hurried on for the occasion. As a story it is hastily put together. An unexpected happening is explained away as being due to " circumstances which we cannot here stop to explain," and at another point we find Maria reduced to writing, " We forgot to mention that . . ." But many of these defects can be attributed to the exceedingly trying conditions under which it was written. In spite of the ebullience of his spirits her father was obviously going through his last illness. (" How I do enjoy my existence," he could be heard exclaiming.) Maria was in great distress of mind. It was at her father's particular request that *Ormond* was written at all and it must have been with mixed pleasure and grief that she read the first chapter to him in the carriage as Edgeworth went out to pay the last visit that he was to pay anywhere. Each subsequent chapter was read aloud to the whole family who gathered round her father's bed to

listen. In spite of his increasing weakness, the warmth of
his appreciation, his suggestions, his comments, his insistence
on writing part of the novel for her revealed that his one
fear, of his mind decaying before his body, was not to be
realised. " When he thought there was spirit in what was
written," Maria wrote of her father's general custom, and
we can be sure that he followed it on his death-bed, " but
that it required correction, he would say, ' Leave that to
me ; it is my business to cut and correct—yours to write
on.' " There is something very solemn in the thought of
Edgeworth's spending his last hours in correcting and even
dictating whole passages of Maria's manuscript. His red face
ran with perspiration, he was in the greatest pain, but he
who had invented walking machines, a one-wheel chaise
and a clock without wheels was determined that the work
of improvement should go on. He knew that he was dying.
It is touching that he should have thought his last hours
could not be spent better than in tracing the adventures of
an Edgeworthian Tom Jones.

For such is Ormond. He is an orphan reared by Sir Ulick
O'Shane but allowed to run wild and consort with game-
keepers and the like. Unlike Vivian, however, he knows
his own mind. He holds himself back from the seduction
of a servant girl because it would grieve her lover. He learns
French and good manners so that when he eventually comes
into an unexpected fortune and turns up in Parisian society
he is a tremendous success. The theme of the book is
how innate qualities will lead a man to triumph over the
deficiencies of education.

Sir Ulick O'Shane and his cousin Mr. Cornelius O'Shane
(or King Corny of the Black Islands as he is more familiarly
known) are not cut to any moral pattern, they are not

manipulated to teach any particular moral lesson, and they must be reckoned among the most successful that Maria ever had to deal with. Sir Ulick is an engaging mixture of warm-heartedness and a keen regard for his own interest ; although he is fonder of Ormond than he is of his own son the moment that he suspects Ormond of supplanting that son in the affections of a certain heiress Ormond is banished from the estate. He goes to King Corny for protection.

The change from Castle Hermitage to the Black Islands is the change from eighteenth-century Ireland to the world of the Odyssey. King Corny is a Homeric king. Within his dominions his word is law and his subjects worship him yet he lives among them simply and, what is more, does not think it beneath his dignity to make himself useful with his hands.

> King Corny had with his own hands made a violin and a rat trap ; and had made the best coat, and the best pair of shoes, and the best pair of boots, and the best hat ; and had knit the best pair of stockings, and had made the best dunghill in his dominions.

But for the fear that his letters might go astray he would have called his castle " the palace." His days are spent in the administration of rough justice (the severest penalty was banishment) hard drinking and hunting with hounds and horn.

" The *first idea* of him," Maria wrote, " was taken from the facts I heard of an oddity, a man I believe like no other, who lived in a remote part of Ireland, an ingenious despot in his own family, who blasted out of the rock on which his house was built half a kitchen, while he and family and guests were living in the house ; who was so passionate that, children, grown up-sons, servants and all, ran out of

6

the house at once when he fell into a passion with his own
tangled hair ; a man who used, in his impatience and rages
to call at the head of the kitchen stairs to the servants, ' Drop
whatever you have in your hand, and come here and be
d——d ! ' He was generous and kindhearted, but despotic
and conceited to the most ludicrous degree : for instance,
he thought he could work gobelins tapestry and play on the
harp or the mandoline better than anyone living. One after
another, in working out King Corny, from the first wrong
hint I was obliged to give up every fact except that he
propped up the roof of his house and built downwards, and
to generalise all ; and to make him a man of expedients,
of ingenious substitutes, such as any clever Irishman in middle
life is used to."

In Maria's opinion fiction should not deal with exceptional
or freakish characters ; they may be amusing and diverting
but they are not edifying. A writer who speaks from
authority (and especially if he is a moralist) as distinct from
the writer whose work is a kind of exploration will naturally
bring out those qualities in his characters which puts them
in line with generally recognised types. What they aim at
is the situation which shall have greater validity than the
merely eccentric, and is more amenable to the formulation of
reasonable laws about human conduct. Dostoevsky stands
at the other extreme. He is the bemused stockman of vast
prairies across which the wild herds range ; the beasts are
always moving outwards from any point of concentration,
a movement that is disruptive to the eye and disturbing
to the imagination. With Maria Edgeworth the cattle are
in their pens, they have been weighed, prodded and sold by
auction before we have even had the opportunity to make
a bid.

What would Dickens have made of King Corny ? Every one of the eccentricities that Maria noted would have been dwelt upon with delight. We should see King Corny at breakfast, his family around him, while the house shook with subterranean explosions as the workmen blasted away in the kitchen. " Drop whatever you have in your hand and come here and be damned," would have been heard fourteen times a day, we should have seen King Corny making his own clothes, giving a concert and riding off to the hunt cracking his great whip and cheering the dogs. The task of making such material sound convincing (and it was on the truth of her stories, on their realism that Maria particularly prided herself) she felt beyond her powers. Had she written her memoirs King Corny would have been there in all his pristine, baroque queerness, " for the value of these odd characters depends, I acknowledge, upon their being actually known to be true. In fiction we have not this *conviction*."

She was probably wise. Fact, like a patch on an old coat, can too easily come away from the fiction it is decorating leaving a greater hole than there was before. But the concealed issue here is not, perhaps, the obvious one to which Henry James made repeated reference : that too much heard of a real happening will ruin the story that could otherwise have been constructed out of the significant hint or suggestion. Maria is not so much concerned with the pearl that her imagination could settle around the grain of fact, nor would she understand the belief (as Henry James would) that if a fact is unbelievable it is the novelist's job to make it acceptable to our belief. Quite apart from the natural tendency of didactic fiction to deal in types and humours there was, tucked away at the back of her mind, a deference to the audience for which she was writing, the aristocracy and landed gentry of England. Knowing that there are limits to what even the best-disposed members of polite society will believe about creatures living outside their magic circle she busied herself in the presentation of characters which though certainly not more true to life were probably more accessible to the imagination of the reading public. Even so, her readers would probably have accepted much more of the joyous extravagance of the original material than she allowed herself to use. The reception given to *Castle Rackrent* should have shown her that.

The Parisian scenes in the novel are brilliantly done. Corny's daughter Dora comes alive in a way that she never did back in the Black Islands. Surrounded by admirers who blazed with crosses and stars she accepted her incense with just the right degree of condescension. Maria was never afraid of the extraordinary or the unusual when it took place in fashionable society. Lady Delacour fighting a duel, Buckhurst Falconer saving a bishop from choking by blowing in his ear, were thought to be quite acceptable to the imagination of the refined reading public ; it was their world and they could be counted upon to understand its vagaries.

Yet the Paris here described was not contemporary Paris, not even the Paris of 1802. It is the Paris of Mr. Edgeworth's younger days, and Maria drew plentifully on his memories of the time. Ormond has the Edgeworth fault, a passionate temper. He has the Edgeworth prudence ; when Edgeworth was in France he decided that five hundred guineas was the precise amount that he could afford to lose at gambling. Once this amount was gone he would play no more. Ormond adopts the same tactics and arouses great admiration on account of his phlegm in the face of his wins and losses. It is Mr. Edgeworth's view of society under Louis XV that is here happily preserved for us and the wonder is that so much comes through the double authorship undimmed.

Three passages of *Ormond* were dictated by Mr. Edgeworth during his last illness. The first was the death of King Corny (a mistake, surely, to kill him off so soon), the second was an account of a jail break in Chapter 30 (about fourteen pages) and the last was the account of Moriarty's meeting with his wife in Chapter 31. We have Maria's authority for this information, the only indication of the precise share taken by her father in any of her writings. In view of what we know of Edgeworth's disposition and his reputation for marring the novels by the interpolation of stretches of dreary moralising it is interesting to examine these three passages to see whether they give support for such a belief. They do nothing of the sort, of course. The story of the jail break is an amusing and lively passage, depending for its humour on the fact that the governor of the jail has promised one of the prisoners a free pardon if he succeeds in escaping—a characteristic Irish situation that Edgeworth obviously relished. No, when it came to the actual revision of Maria's texts Edgeworth's influence was probably all for liveliness and economy. " He corrected *Ormond* many, many times," said Maria, " often working at it in his bed for hours together—once at the end for six hours, between the intervals of sickness and exquisite pain."

On May 31, being his birthday, he rose from his bed, dressed and ordered the carriage to be brought round to the door. He took three sons and Maria with him on his drive

Maria, as they went along, read passages from *Ormond* to him until they reached the market town where Mr. Edgeworth's eloquence was soon heard (for Maria had stopped reading, not being able to compete with the squealing of the pigs and the neighing of the horses) ringing above the clamour. He died a fortnight later and Maria said that she felt as if she had lived to a remote old age.

When *Ormond* was published there was the customary preface by Mr. Edgeworth :

> And now, indulgent reader, I beg you to pardon this intrusion, and, with the most grateful acknowledgements, I bid you farewell for ever.
>
> RICHARD LOVELL EDGEWORTH.
> EDGEWORTH'S TOWN,
>   *May* 31, 1817.

Although Maria lived for over thirty years after the death of her father she wrote only one more considerable work of fiction, *Helen,* and this did not begin to occupy her imagination until 1830. In the meantime a great deal of pious literary work had to be done. First and foremost there was the autobiographical fragment that her father had left with the injunction that she was to complete it. It was a task on which Maria spent more worry and love than on any other literary work. She felt that she was " drifting over an unknown sea, without chart or compass," her eye troubles of childhood recurred and at one time it was thought that she might lose her sight, but the great effort was made, the memoirs were completed (her sisters helping by copying or writing from dictation) and published in 1820.

The first volume, written by Edgeworth himself, makes very much the better reading, partly because it is a lively record of an eighteenth-century progressive mind, but mainly for the very quality that so offended the *Quarterly Review*, the belief of the author that the details of his career, being of such vast interest to himself, must necessarily be of vast interest to everyone else. Much of the material is valuable in itself, especially the bland portrait of Thomas Day and as such would naturally be seized upon by any memoir writer. But only Edgeworth would have thought it worth while to give an account of the clergyman living in strict retirement with a young goddess whose bosom, Edgeworth records, was " of that healthful whiteness which admits of no comparison with any inaminate object in creation." On the lawn in front of the house there was a model of the solar system, the sun and the larger planets being made of lath and plaster, the smaller globes of plaster of paris. " I scarcely ventured to make further enquiries about this gentleman," Edgeworth wrote cautiously.

For many years Maria had enjoyed a European reputation and when she decided to visit Paris and Switzerland in 1820, taking her two young sisters Fanny and Harriet with her, she received a welcome that left in her memory the impression of a dream of " Alps and glaciers and cascades, and Mont Blanc, and troops of acquaintance in splendid succession and visionary confusion." In the years to come there were other voyages and excursions, to London principally, to Scotland where Maria stayed at Abbotsford, and, a momentous occasion, a trip to the wilds of Connemara which produced an immensely long letter to a stepbrother in India that makes quite as good reading as the Irish passages in her tales. But the great experience of these later years was, of course, Scott. For Maria he was " the most perfectly agreeable and perfectly amiable great man I ever knew "—and, as far as Scott was concerned, Lockhart said that the period

of Maria's visit to Abbotsford was one of the happiest of
his life. It was quite impossible, said Scott, that before
writing one of her stories Maria did not produce a wand
and conjure for a little while. The visit was repaid in 1825,
Scott bringing with him his daughter, his son and daughter-
in-law and Lockhart. It was the last real holiday of Scott's
life and he was, in Maria's words, " the noblest and gentlest
of lions." She was proud to think that posterity would
remember her as his friend ; it would be enough for her if
she were remembered for no other reason. During the stay
the whole party went on a trip to Killarney and twenty
years afterwards a boatman told Macaulay that the pleasure
of rowing them quite made up for missing a hanging that
day. Within a few months Messrs. Constable and Ballantyne
failed and Maria never saw her hero again.

For the last eight years the management of the Edgeworth
estates had been in the hands of Lovell, the " wise and
economic Lovell " as his father had called him. He had
been a *détenu* for twelve years in France and since his release
had been mainly occupied in setting up a school in the village
that would put his father's educational ideas into practice.
But he was a child in money matters and the once-prosperous
Edgeworth estates were heading downhill so rapidly that
Maria had to intervene and pack off Lovell to live in England
on remittances. By a shrewdness and prudence that one
would hardly have expected of Rosamond, borrowing
money here, repaying there, and all the time refusing to
sell land, the estate was saved. But it was work, of course,
that left her very little time for writing.

In 1830 we find her thinking out *Helen* over her needle-
work. It was a task to which she set herself with the very
greatest diffidence, feeling nervously incapable of grappling

once more with the familiar perils of the imagination, but this time without her father's support. There was no point, it seemed, in producing a formal plan of campaign when her father was not there to run his eye over it. The work proceeded under the guidance of what she hoped would be spontaneous promptings and the result is a sprawling formlessness in the novel that makes one almost wish for Mr. Edgeworth's supervisory cutting. It was not a novel about Ireland. That was impossible, said Maria, " It is impossible to draw Ireland as she now is in a book of fiction —realities are too strong, party passions too violent to bear to see, or to look at their faces in the looking glass. The people would only break the glass and curse the fool who held the mirror up to nature—distorted nature in a fever. We are in too perilous a case to laugh, humour would be out of season, worse than bad taste."

We are, accordingly, set down in a spacious, English country house where the imagination need not be affrighted by reality. This does not mean that the English scene was chosen as a means of escaping into the consolations of the past. *Helen* looks forward, not backwards.

It would be an exaggeration to say that she faced up to what has always been the general criticism of her writings, that they are too often her moral tales for children in adult dress. It was a quality for which the *Quarterly Review*, in comparing her with Jane Austen, had administered public rebuke. Yet she had given much thought to the most effective way of disguising what, at the age of sixty, she knew to be the inevitable spring of her imagination. " How difficult it is to introduce the moral into a story," she had said to Walter Scott, and he had replied that the rats would not go into the trap if they could smell the hand of the rat-catcher. One of the qualities for which she admired Scott was his ability to weave his moral into the texture of the story. Inevitably she came to regard the concealment of the moral as one of the supreme tests of the novelist's art.

" We must take leave to pause for one moment to remark," we find her writing with engaging transparency in *Helen*, " not in the way of moralising, by any means, but simply as a matter of history, that the first little fib in which Lady Cecilia, as a customary license of speech, indulged herself the moment she awoke this morning, though it seemed to answer its purpose exactly at the time, occasioned her ladyship a good deal of superfluous toil and trouble during the course of the day." Lady Cecilia's fondness for fibbing her way out of difficulties is the hard core of the novel, but it is not, as well it might be had *Helen* been one of the *Tales of Fashionable Life*, the only spark of individuality that her ladyship possesses. She is an agreeable, generous and high-spirited girl who, before her marriage, did not think flirtation any more than a pleasant pastime. And as though to give Cecilia some sort of justification for her disposition Maria provided her with a husband, General Clarendon, who turns out to be a domestic tyrant worthy of Miss Compton-Burnett. Maria only goes so far as to admit that " he had made up his fagot of opinions and would not let one stick be drawn out for examination lest he should loosen the whole bundle," but to anyone with less austere views on human conduct the General seems to be the sort of impossible creature to whom a wife would have to lie as one of her natural means of defence. As a bachelor he had taken the pompous decision that he would never marry a woman who had previously been in love. The modern reader, while deploring that the sprightly Cecilia should ever have married such a stick, is tempted to applaud her good sense in not telling the General that she has not been fancy-free in the interval between "coming-out" and meeting him. But the situation is genuine, so far from being alienated from Cecilia by her little weakness (as we are alienated from so many of Maria's walking embodiments of human imperfection) she has our sympathies. We should have no reproaches but for the suspicion that General Clarendon's conduct has an unfair share of Maria's approval. One of the surest signs of a novel's "dating" is our inability to accept the characters at the author's assessment, or the assessment of the author's contemporaries.

And what of the heights, the wellnigh inaccessible, cold, pure heights of the heroine herself? Helen is a refreshing contrast to the self-contained heroines of so many of the earlier novels. Although there is no romantic woolliness about her character (she is bold enough to tackle the general himself when she feels that he is treating her unfairly) she is imprudent enough to get into debt and human enough to fall in love with the hero without the circumspection and calculation that we have come to expect. Beauclerk himself is a real young man, intolerably so at times, with a few sillinesses and a fair share of bad manners. But we must not exaggerate. Beauclerk, as a creation, is no improvement on Clarence Hervey of *Belinda*. Even the incident of Helen's getting into debt over a piece of extravagance bears the air of contrivance, rather as though the authoress had said, "I must avoid negative perfection at all costs." We cannot help wishing that we were given less of Helen and her Beauclerk and a little more of such people as Miss Clarendon who said precisely what she thought even at the most inconvenient moments ; or Lady Bearcroft who had "risen

above her station " and thought she could enliven the rather
dull proceedings of the house-party by producing a packet
of vulgar political cartoons. They were received in shocked
silence. " The world is grown mighty nice," Lady Bearcroft
remarked, " For my part give me a good laugh when it's to
be had."

The interminable dullness of those country house-parties !
It is always midsummer and the would-be brilliant conversation beats out morning, afternoon and evening, resolving
such questions as the true nature of a sense of punctuality
and how it differs from a slavish observance of ceremony.
Fans are raised in the warm air to conceal the inevitable
yawn, watches are fondled in anticipation of the gong for
the next meal. But when Lady Davenant appears, the
atmosphere is changed, the conversation moves round to
new topics and we forget the smell of cooking that is being
wafted along the elegant corridors. Just as *Patronage* is
dominated by and memorable for Lord Oldborough, so
Helen is to be remembered for Lady Davenant, who might
well have been his younger sister.

There had been intellectual and intelligent women in
fiction before, there had been wit and sparkling conversation,
there had been women of powerful and even domineering
character. But Lady Davenant represents one of the first
attempts to put a female politician into a novel. There had
been nothing in English public life to compare with the
petticoat politics that flourished on the other side of the
Channel—it was in emulation of such examples that Lady
Davenant originally stirred herself—and even in Maria's
new character we see nothing of the power that could shape
policies, could make and break statesmen. Lady Davenant's
ascendancy is entirely moral and intellectual. Had she lived

to-day she would have been a Cabinet Minister ; in the
1830's she was the wife of an Ambassador. She had a
political *salon*, her love of power had (through experience)
been tempered by justice, her favourite reading was a
government Blue book, and she was never happier than when
discussing such subjects as the distress of the Polish refugees.
As a character of fiction she is new in this sense. Just as
Maria herself had become increasingly concerned in the
affairs of Ireland so Lady Davenant found that political issues
were occupying her to the exclusion of more fashionable
acquirements. " You cannot expect, Helen," she said,
" that you, as a rational being, can go through the world
as it now is without forming any opinion on points of
public importance. You cannot, I conceive, satisfy yourself
with the common namby-pamby, little-missy phrase, ' ladies
have nothing to do with politics.' " Whereas Lady Delacour
neglected her daughter because family life interfered with
her social success Lady Davenant neglected her daughter
Cecilia for the affairs of Europe.

Maria was looking ahead. She, who had been one of the
first to greet Dr. Erasmus Darwin's *Botanic Garden*, was
reading Peacock, Dickens and Balzac. Rosamond had
indeed made great progress.

She enjoyed such a long, such a happy and such a successful
life that if to all this had been added the art of a Jane Austen
it would have been altogether unfair. But with Jane Austen
as the standard to measure her by we have, of course,
demanded nothing less. It explains, in part, why the
novels of Maria Edgeworth are neglected and unread. The
common reader has a way of looking at the novelists of the
past that is different from the critic's. He looks for pleasures
that are more immediate than the realisation that whereas

Jane Austen was so much the better novelist Maria Edgeworth may be the more important. For whereas Jane Austen
surveyed with the eye of a realist ground that had already been
tilled, and brought it to perfection, Maria struck out and sub-
dued stretches of new territory, the psychology of children,
the dignified and humorous mind of the peasant, the resolute
mind of a woman of affairs, and she supplied an impetus for
the writing of all regional fiction, for Scott in Scotland, for
Fenimore Cooper in America, for Turgenev in Russia.

Her stepmother, who first collected Maria's letters and
printed them, has left a portrait of Maria as she was in later
years. Throughout her long life roses had seemed in
perpetual blow. Rosamond was the name under which
she concealed her own identity in her stories ; roses had
greeted her arrival at Edgeworthstown in 1782 and now, in
later years, American admirers sent her hampers of them in
the fast packet. She rose early and came in to breakfast
with an armful of dew-drenched blossoms to decorate the
table. She ate little for breakfast but enjoyed it immensely,
knitting as she talked or read aloud from her letters. There
were manuscripts from young writers to look over, letters
to write appealing for funds and food to meet the distress
that was so soon to grow into the great famine. For two
hours every morning, then, she worked away at her desk,
a true Edgeworth desk with brackets, screens, compartments,
gadgets—and a pen that was presented to her by a certain
celebrated guest.

" I am such a minikin lion now," she said, " and so old,
literally without teeth or claws."

Whenever she spoke of lions we know that she was
thinking of Sir Walter Scott.

She died on May 22nd, 1849, in her eighty-third year.

BIBLIOGRAPHY

Memoirs of Richard Lovell Edgeworth, Esq., begun by himself and concluded by his daughter Maria Edgeworth. 2 vols. London, 1820.

Life and Letters of Maria Edgeworth. Edited by her friends. 3 vols. F. A. Edgeworth, 1867. (Printed but not published. The source of most of our information. A copy is in the British Museum.)

The Life and Letters of Maria Edgeworth. AUGUSTUS HARE. 2 vols. London, 1894. (Selections from the 1867 volumes.)

Maria Edgeworth. (Eminent Women Series.) HELEN ZIMMERN. London, 1882.

Maria Edgeworth. (English Men of Letters Series.) Hon. EMILY LAWLESS. London, 1904.

Maria Edgeworth and her Circle in the days of Bonaparte and Bourbon. CONSTANCE HILL. London, 1910.

The Edgeworths: A Study in later Eighteenth-Century Education. ALICE PATERSON. London, 1914.

The Black Book of Edgeworthstown. Edited by Harriet Jessie Butler and Harold Edgeworth Butler. London, 1927.

Maria Edgeworth: Chosen Letters. Edited by F. V. Barry. London, 1931. (Contains some letters not available in the volumes of 1867 and 1894.)

A Century of Children's Books. F. V. BARRY. London, 1922.

The Popular Novel in England, 1770–1800. J. M. S. TOMKINS, London, 1932.

NOVELS AND STORIES BY
MARIA EDGEWORTH (1767–1849)

1796. *The Parent's Assistant.*

1800. *Castle Rackrent.*

1801. *Early Lessons.*

1801. *Moral Tales.*

1801. *Belinda.*

1804. *Popular Tales.*

1805. *The Modern Griselda.*

1806. *Leonora.*

1809. *Tales of Fashionable Life* (First Series : *Ennui, Almeria, The Dun, Manœuvering*).

1812. *Tales of Fashionable Life* (Second Series : *Vivian, Emilie de Coulanges, The Absentee*).

1814. *Early Lessons* (continued).

1814. *Patronage.*

1817. *Harrington.*

1817. *Ormond.*

1817. *Comic Dramas.*

1821. *Rosamond, a sequel to Early Lessons.*

1822. *Frank, a sequel to Early Lessons.*

1825. *Harry and Lucy, conclusion to Early Lessons.*

1827. *Little Plays for Children.*

1834. *Helen.*

1848. *Orlandino.*

INDEX

A Selection of Press Notices about

THE ENGLISH NOVELISTS SERIES

6s. each

" To introduce, to sum up ; that is the ticklish double purpose contributors have to observe. With the first two volumes Miss Phyllis Bentley and Mr. G. D. H. Cole set a very high standard indeed."—G. W. Stonier in *The Observer*.

" This book (THE BRONTËS) is the first of a new series entitled ' The English Novelists ' which, if the high standard set by Miss Bentley be maintained, should be valuable."—Elizabeth Bowen in *The Tatler*.

" The series is delightfully produced and printed, each book running to about 115 pages of vivid text. This series will be welcomed in the home library, but it is eminently suitable for schools and one could imagine it forming a first-class background series for a course of lessons."—*Schoolmaster*.

64763

[P.T.O.

" When the publishers of this new series of critical biographies, or monographs, of great English novelists declare that there is now a special need for interest in English literature, and for a vigorous criticism and appreciation to be kept alive, there can be nothing but applause for such recognition of the plight into which the craft of letters, the work of education, and general critical alertness have been thrown by official sanction of the nation, after a war to extirpate it, that exercise of the mind is of comparative unimportance in life. For the time being we have to rely, by Government order, on home production. The publishers' aim is thus to be welcomed, and they make a happy start in works by Miss Phyllis Bentley and Mr. G. D. H. Cole."—*The Times Literary Supplement.*

" There is room for the new series of volumes discussing the English novelists."—*Northern Whig.*

" The excellent series on the English novelists."—*Church of England newspaper.*

[P.T.O.

" Both Phyllis Bentley's introduction to THE BRONTËS, and G. D. H. Cole's to the work of SAMUEL BUTLER promise well for the new—and most pleasingly produced—series they launch."—*John o' London's Weekly*.

" A matter for some literary excitement."—*Irish Times*.

" This new series promises writers of a challenging sort, ' people of vigorous and sometimes extremely unorthodox mind.' "—*Notes and Queries*.

" Such a series is an admirable idea and answers a need."—J. S. Collis in *Time and Tide*.

[P.T.O.

THE BRONTËS (*Fourth Impression*) **By Phyllis Bentley**
" Miss Bentley's account of the novels and the poems is perspicacious criticism, meriting the attention of the general reader and the literary student."—*The Times Literary Supplement.*

SAMUEL BUTLER **By G. D. H. Cole**
" This new volume makes an excellent introduction to Butler the novelist."—Paul Bloomfield in the *New Statesman.*

HENRY FIELDING **By Elizabeth Jenkins**
" Miss Jenkins' study is intelligent, sympathetic and well written."—V. S. Pritchett in the *New Statesman.*

ROBERT LOUIS STEVENSON **By Lettice Cooper**
" Miss Cooper has done an excellent piece of work." —Philip Trower in the *Spectator.*

RUDYARD KIPLING **By Rupert Croft-Cooke**
" This study is sympathetic, sensible and discerning." —Bonamy Dobrée in the *Spectator.*

BULWER-LYTTON **By the Earl of Lytton, K.G.**
"This skilful epitome."—Michael Sadleir in the *Sunday Times.*

ARNOLD BENNETT **By Walter Allen**
" I think that it is the best study of Bennett that has ever been made."—Howard Spring in *Country Life.*

SIR WALTER SCOTT **By Una Pope-Hennessy**
" The knowledge behind it is extensive."—*Yorkshire Post.*

MRS. GASKELL **By Yvonne ffrench**
" . . . this essay is a fine and accomplished little work, abounding in shrewdness and subtlety of observation." —C. E. Vulliamy in the *Spectator.*

Date Due